BLACK MASK

&

UP AGAINST THE WALL MOTHERFUCKER

BLACK MASK

&

UP AGAINST THE WALL MOTHERFUCKER

THE INCOMPLETE WORKS OF RON HAHNE, BEN MOREA, AND THE BLACK MASK GROUP

PM PRESS

2011

ISBN: 978-1-60486-021-4
Library of Congress Control Number: 2008921772
Copyright © 2011 Ben Morea and Ron Hahne
This edition copyright © 2011 PM Press

PM Press
PO Box 23912
Oakland, CA 94623
www.pmpress.org

Printed in the United States on recycled paper.

Cover and new edition design: Josh MacPhee | justseeds.org
Cover photographer unknown

TABLE OF CONTENTS

They say hindsight is 20/20. How about foresight? Change is what we sought, and change is what we got. America was split 80/20 in favor of Vietnam but NOW 80/20 against Iraq. The Great Movement for social change in the '60s (of which Black Mask and U.A.W./M.F.were part) is still in the air. Only resolve is lacking. Its time shall come. Only inertia keeps the status/quo in place. Look for the Green. Look for the BLACK. Never lose HOPE.

—Ben Morea

SECTION ONE

BLACK MASK
ISSUES 1-10

BLACK MASK

No. 1   NOV. 1966   5 Cents

A new spirit is rising. Like the streets of Watts we burn with revolution. We assault your Gods - - We sing of your death. DESTROY THE MUSEUMS - - our struggle cannot be hung on walls. Let the past fall under the blows of revolt. The guerilla, the blacks, the men of the future, we are all at your heels. Goddamn your culture, your science, your art. What purpose do they serve? Your mass-murder cannot be concealed. The industrialist, the banker, the bourgeoisie, with their unlimited pretense and vulgarity, continue to stockpile art while they slaughter humanity. Your lie has failed. The world is rising against your oppression. There are men at the gates seeking a new world. The machine, the rocket, the conquering of space and time, these are the seeds of the future which, freed from your barbarism, will carry us forward. We are ready - -

LET THE STRUGGLE BEGIN.

BLACK MASK No. 1 - November 1966

A new spirit is rising. Like the streets of Watts we burn with revolution. We assault your Gods... We sing of your death. DESTROY THE MUSEUMS... our struggle cannot be hung on walls. Let the past fall under the blows of revolt. The guerrilla, the blacks, the men of the future, we are all at your heels. Goddamn your culture, your science, your art. What purpose do they serve? Your mass-murder cannot be concealed. The industrialist, the banker, the bourgeoisie, with their unlimited pretence and vulgarity, continue to stockpile art while they slaughter humanity. Your lie has failed. The world is rising against your oppression. There are men at the gates seeking a new world. The machine, the rocket, the conquering of space and time, these are the seeds of the future which, freed from your barbarism, will carry us forward. We are ready...

LET THE STRUGGLE BEGIN.

The statement on the first page was issued as part of an action taken against the Museum of Modern Art. The accompanying press release was meant as a partial explanation.

On Monday, October 10 at 12.30pm we will close the Museum of Modern Art. This symbolic action is taken at a time when America is on a path of total destruction, and signals the opening of another front in the world-wide struggle against suppression. We seek a total revolution, cultural, as well as social and political - LET THE STRUGGLE BEGIN.

A number of copies were also sent via the mail, in response to which we received the following letter. For further clarification of our ideas and actions we publish both the letter and our response.

Dear Friends:

The scribbling on your leaflet enclosed was my immediate reaction ("why mess with this - close the War Plants, or the Pentagon or City Hall, or the Precinct Station") but George thinks it's too blunt and tactless. I don't agree really: I expect revolutionaries to be thick-skinned enough to stand rough treatment without confusing their friends with their enemies. But he's too busy right now to write to you himself.

Thanks for sending the stuff - tho I couldn't disagree more, I hope you'll keep us on your mailing list, and we'll add you to ours.

But why oh why start with the museums??? If you want to assault the gods, attack religion; if you want to end the slaughter, attack the war machine; if you oppose oppression, attack the state. Or is it really only the pretence and vulgarity - not the power - of the bourgeoisie that bugs you? If so, it's not enough to build a revolution on. The man-power it takes to overthrow a system won't come from the small minority of us that are concerned with culture; it'll come from the mass oppressed by power. And most of them don't give a damn whether the Museum of Modern Art is open or closed, or whether it exists at all; their problems are much more vital, like whether they're going to die in Vietnam or from a cop's bullet in the back. Like the waste of their passionate youth in the stultifying routine of classrooms decades behind the world they're growing into. Like having to sell their humanity in eight-hour slices to pay rent and the groceries - and not even because production any longer needs it, but just because it's what the wielders of power decree.

Sure: LET THE STRUGGLE BEGIN. But let's not just nip at their heels, let's strike where it really hurts!

Love

Louise Crowley

Dear Louise:

It is possible that the red-ink of your "immediate reaction' prevented you from reading our statement (if so, another is enclosed) but assuming you did read it, I hope a few comments will help clear up some of your misunderstandings.

Your first question is "why start with the museums." I assume you mean why do we start with museums, since no where do we say that others should start here, or for that matter that they should abandon their present course to join us, in fact quite to the contrary we state that we are going to join them, by "opening another front." We fully realize the manpower it takes to overthrow a system won't come from a small minority but we are not a small minority since we are joining a world-wide struggle, which has many fronts.

As creative men, we say "destroy the museums" yet we are no more interested in closing the Modern Art than you are, it is instead symbolic to us of the total suppression of man. Why does the ghetto dweller attack the slumlord instead of the more powerful bankers behind them or the capitalist system itself? Because a man strikes at that which directly confronts him. We don't question this action, yet as revolutionaries we hope it is taken with knowledge of the total picture or that it will at least lead to a deeper understanding. Yet you question us, as creative men, for attacking the museums. You must have realized that we saw this as part of a wider struggle since we linked ourselves to the "guerrilla" and the "blacks" and quite literally stated "we seek a total revolution, cultural as well as social and political."

I assume then that you question the relevance of a cultural revolution as part of wider revolution. The fact that you think only a small minority is concerned with culture is part of a basic misconception, which equates culture with western-bourgeois culture. The Vietnamese are fighting against the destruction of their culture as well as their land. The African revolutionaries have always been concerned with the preservation of their culture in the face of colonialism. And in this country the black man is becoming more aware of his culture, among others, the birth of jazz being no mean achievement. As well as the Mexican, Puerto Rican and Indian seeking to preserve theirs.

Obviously, none of these people are concerned with museums, but neither are we (other than seeing them destroyed). They are involved with a living culture which is what we hope to see rise throughout America, a living culture which comes from the creative spirit of man. With this we can change the stultifying classrooms, the inhuman city, the concept of work when it is unnecessary and everything else which is crushing life instead of allowing it to grow fully. This cannot be achieved without revolution, but neither can it be achieved without the creative force. Sure: Close the warplants or the pentagon or city hall or the precinct station - but don't stop there, let their culture fall too. FF

Albert Camus: Interview in Demain;
Issue 24, — 30 Oct. 1957

The notion of art for art's sake is obviously alien to your thinking. That of "Commitment" as it has been made fashionable of late is equally so. Taken in its present meaning, commitment consists in making one's own art subservient to a policy. It seems to me that there is something more important, which is characteristic of your work, that might be called inserting that work into its time. Is this correct? And if it is, how would you describe that insertion?

I can accept your expression: inserting a work into its time. But, after all, this describes all literary art. Every writer tries to give a form to the passions of his time. Yesterday it was love. Today the great passions of unity and liberty disrupt the world. Yesterday love led to individual death. Today collective passions make us run the risk of universal destruction. Today just as yesterday, art wants to save from death a living image of our passions and our suffering.

Perhaps it is harder today. It is possible to fall in love every once in a while. Once is enough, after all. But it is not possible to be a militant in one's spare time. And so the artist of today becomes unreal if he remains in his ivory tower or sterilized if he spends his time galloping around the political arena. Yet between the two lies the arduous way of true art. It seems to me that the writer must be fully aware of the dramas of his time and that he must take sides every time he can or knows how to do so. He must also maintain, or resume from time to time a certain distance in relation to our history. Every work presupposes a content of reality and a creator who shapes the container. Consequently, the artist, if he must share the misfortune of his time, must also tear himself away in order to consider that misfortune and give it form. This continual shuttling, this tension that gradually becomes increasingly dangerous, is the task of the artist today. Perhaps this means that in a short time there will be no more artists. And perhaps not. It is a question of time, of strength of mastery and also of chance.

In any case, this is what ought to be. There remains what is; there remains the truth of our days which is less magnificent. And the truth, as I see it at least, is that the artist is groping his way in the dark, just like the man in the street — incapable of separating himself from the world's misfortune and passionately longing for solitude and silence; dreaming of justice, yet being himself a source of injustice; dragged — even though he thinks he is driving it — behind a chariot that is bigger than he. In this exhausting adventure the artist can only draw help from others, and, like anyone else, he will get help from pleasure, from forgetting, and also from friendship and admiration. And like anyone else, he will get help from hope. In my case, I have always drawn my hope from the idea of fecundity. Like many men Today, I am tired of criticism, of disparagement, of spitefulness — and of nihilism in short. It is essential to condemn what must be condemned, but swiftly and firmly. On the other hand, one should praise at length what deserves to be praised. After all, that is why I am an artist, because even the work that negates still affirms something and does homage to the wretched and magnificent life that is ours.

When a man speaks as you do, he is not solely speaking for himself. He is inevitably speaking for others. And he is speaking for something. In other words, he is speaking in the name of and in the favour of men for whom those values count. Who are those men and what are those values.

To begin with, I feel a solidarity with the common man. Tomorrow the world may burst into fragments. In that threat hanging over our heads there is a lesson of truth. As we face such a future, heirarchies, titles, honors are reduced to what they are in reality: a passing puff of smoke. And the only certainty left to us is that of naked suffering, common to all, intermingling its roots with those of stubborn hope.

In all your work there co-exist philosophical pessimism and, nonetheless, not optimism but a sort of confidence. Confidence in the spirit rather than in man, in nature rather than in the universe, in action rather than in its results. Do you think this attitude — which is that of the rebel, for the value of the revolt makes up for the world's absurdity — can be adopted by the majority or is it condemned to remain the privilege of a few wise men?

Is that position really so special? And do not the men of today, threatened and yet resisting, live in this manner? We stifle and yet survive, we think we are dying of grief and yet life wins out. The men of our time, whom we encounter in the streets, show in their faces that they know. The only difference is that some of them show more courage. Besides, we have no choice. It is either that or nihilism, whether totalitarian or bourgeois, then those individuals who refuse to give in will stand apart, and they must accept this. But in their place and within their means, they must do what is necessary so that all can live together.

Personally, I have never wanted to stand apart. For the man of today there is a sort of solitude, which is certainly the harshest thing our era forces upon us. I feel its weight, believe me. But, nevertheless, I should not want to change eras, for I also know and respect the greatness of this one. Moreover, I have always thought that the maximum danger implied the maximum hope.

Power Concedes Nothing Without A Demand

'Find out just what any people will quietly submit to and you have found out the exact measure of injustice and wrong which will be imposed upon them, and these will continue till they are resisted with either words or blows or both.'

For many years black people in the black belt of Alabama have been the victims of a vicious system of political, economic and social exclusion. Political exclusion is maintained in many ways — the denial of the right to vote, service on juries, access to political offices and by naked brutality acting under color of law or just a plain white sheet.

Although black people are a numerical majority of Lowndes County, Alabama the Democratic Party only provides them with white candidates who will adhere to a policy of white supremacy. The Lowndes County Freedom Organization wants a politics that is responsive to the needs of the poor — responsive to the need for education, decent law enforcement, paved roads, decent housing, good medical facilities, and all the things they hope for themselves and their children.

On November 8th, black people in Lowndes County will have a chance to cast ballots for candidates representing these interests. These candidates running under the symbol of the Black Panther, if elected, will be in positions of control. These will be black people in control, seeking to use the county governing mechanism for the benefit of all persons in Lowndes County. THIS POLITICAL EFFORT IS SIGNIFICANT FOR BLACK PEOPLE AROUND THE COUNTRY, NOT JUST IN LOWNDES COUNTY. THIS EFFORT NEEDS THE SUPPORT OF ALL BLACK PEOPLE.

WHAT YOU CAN DO TO HELP

The Lowndes County Freedom Organization will need money for gasoline to make sure that everyone gets out to vote on November 8th. Candidates need money to help in the canvassing of the county between now and November 8th.

The word needs to be spread about what is happening in Lowndes County.

On election day support rallies should be held for the people of Lowndes County.

Vote fraud or violent assault against the Lowndes County Freedom Organization on election day is a real possibility. Some form of action may be necessary. You may be called on to help.

A VICTORY FOR THE LOWNDES COUNTY FREEDOM ORGANIZATION IS A VICTORY FOR US.

'The whole history of the progress of human liberty shows that all concessions yet made to her .... have been born of earnest struggle.

If there is no struggle there is no progress. Those who profess to favor freedom yet deprecate agitaion, are men who want crops without plowing up the ground, they want rain without thunder and lightning. They want the ocean without the roar of it's many waters.

This struggle may be a moral one, or it may be a physical one, and it may be both moral and physical, but it must be a struggle.

SNCC   LOWNDES COUNTY
360 Nelson St. S.W.   · FREEDOM ORGANIZATION
Atlanta, Georgia 30313   Rte. 1, Box 191
Phone — 404 688-0331   Hayneville, Alabama

BLACK MASK

No. 2   DEC. 1966   5 Cents

The Total Revolution

One continuing purpose of this newsletter will be to fuse fractionalized struggles into a functional whole. Too long we have witnessed the weakening and eventual destruction of radical movements by their forced specialization. Obviously one must function within an area of personal confrontation be it the factory, the ghetto, or the university, but there must always be the inner direction of a totality.

The labor unions concern only with wages and working conditions has all but emasculated their original radicalism. The negro movement for integration would have fallen into the same trap, but now the cry of "Black Power" will put an emphasis on community control, revitalizing their struggle, just as the goal of workers control of production, especially under the impending changes of automation and cybernation,

BLACK MASK No. 2 - December 1966

The Total Revolution

One continuing purpose of this newsletter will be to fuse factionalized struggles into a functional whole. Too long we have witnessed the weakening and eventual destruction of radical movements by their forced specialization. Obviously one must function within an area of personal confrontation be it the factory, the ghetto, or the university, but there must always be the inner direction of a totality. The labor unions' concern only with wages and working conditions has all but emasculated their original radicalism. The negro movement for integration would have fallen into the same trap, but now the cry of "Black Power" will put an emphasis on community control, revitalizing their struggle, just as the goal of workers' control of production, especially under the impending changes of automation and cybernation, would do for the rank and file (assuring them of a voice when labor is no longer necessary and impeding the rise of the welfare state).

As creative men we must seek a similar change, which joined with the struggles of others will bring about the total revolution. We cannot be concerned only with the aesthetic revolution, because without a wider change it will come to nothing. The revolutionary urge of the creative man has always been a part of his desire for a deeper understanding of life and the forces which affect it, but without a concentrated effort at changing the negative forces directly, he will never see his vision realized. We have seen Van Gogh's dedication to life and his deep attachment to the common man completely subverted. Now his work is isolated from life, forced to hang in a musty museum or worse yet the homes of the rich. The same has happened to that American artist who effected one of the most radical aesthetic changes of our time, Jackson Pollock. Not only has his work been made to serve the aggrandizement of the bourgeoisie, but the respect he accrued for American art has been used to sell "Coca-Cola" to the world. Art has become another tool of the imperialist.

We can see this same failure in a movement which even more directly sought to join art and life. The German Bauhaus, founded by Gropius in 1919, had at its roots the need for a creative community to function within society and help transform it to a high aesthetic level. This experiment was crushed by Hitler's rise to power but its effectiveness has been constantly drained by a capitalist criteria, rather than human needs. We can see this more clearly in America, where after its forced exile from Germany, similar ideas and programs were initiated by Moholy-Nagy at the Chicago Institute of Design. The American reality took the ideas of standardization and simplification, and turned them into an excuse for sterilization and dehumanization.

The aesthetic revolution of today must be a part of the total revolution. A revolution which will bring about a society where the arts will be an integral part of life, as in primitive society, and not an appendage to wealth. A society where man has control of his life and the economic wealth of his community. A society free of bureaucracy, both totalitarian and bourgeois. A society where "to each according to his needs" is the rule, not the exception.

B. M.

The following are excerpts from groups which seem to be moving in the same direction (anticipated by the Dadaists and Surrealists), and reflect its universal presence. These few selection are not meant to be a complete listing, since there are other groups both nationally and internationally which have similar tendencies.

Situationist Internationale: Paris

The same society of alienation, of totalitarian control of spectacular consumption reigns everywhere in spite of the variations in the ideological or juridical disguises. The connecting factor in this system of society cannot be understood without an overall criticism in which its opposite is pointed out; the project of free creativity, project of the dominion of all men over their history on every level. This is the demand in deeds of all the proletarian revolutions, demands until now vanquished by the specialists of power who take charge of the revolutions, and make them their private property.

Heatwave: London

Put in different terms, it is the concept of total revolution which has been lost. It has degenerated into a theory of the rectification of economic and political structures, whereas all the most radical periods of the past revolutionary movement were animated by the desire to transform the whole nature of human experience, to create a world in which the desires of each individual could be realized without restriction... Finally to create the revolutionary praxis by which this society and this civilization can be destroyed, once and for all.

Rebel Worker: Chicago

More than ever, with everything continually at stake, we find it necessary to affirm the impassioned use of the most dangerous weapons in the arsenal of freedom MAD LOVE: Totally subversive, the absolute enemy of bourgeois culture. POETRY: (as opposed to literature) breathing like a machine gun, exterminating the blind flags of immediate reality. HUMOR: the dynamite and guerrilla warfare of the mind, as effective in its own domain as material dynamite and guerilla warfare in the streets (when necessary, however rest assured, we shall use every means at our disposal.) SABOTAGE: ruthless and relentless destruction of the bureaucratic and cultural machinery of repression. It is necessary at times (and this is one of them) to speak bluntly: we affirm deliriously and simply the total liberation of man.

Resurgence Youth Movement: NYC

The messianic vision of a total revolution that would transform every social relationship, would erase the concept of Worker as it would the concept of Capitalist, was carried by a minority in the radical movement, Anarchists, Syndicalists, and the recurring heretics of the spirit who ambushed European culture in the 20's and 30's in surrealism... A restatement of this revolutionary theory is a restatement of Anarchist theory. The ideologies of Socialism and Communism are unable to face the development of a totally free revolution. The revolution that we propose is a mind revolution, a body revolution, a soul revolution.

L.Moholy-Nagy: Vision in Motion (1947)

The true artist is the grindstone of the senses; he sharpens eyes, mind and feeling; he interprets ideas and concepts through his own media. In the midst of vast social controversies he cannot escape that task. He has to take sides and proclaim his stand; indeed the artist has a formative ideological function, otherwise his work would be only an exercise of skill in composition. Hitler was aware of this. He propagandized trash, he tried to destroy modern art, science, and philosophy as the greatest sources of opposition to his vicious system of oppression. He banned the contemporary, the "degenerate" art, as he called it from the galleries and museums, burned books, and forbade the teaching of Einstein's theories.

He sensed the content of art is basically not different from the content of our other utterances. The only difference is that art is produced mainly by subconcious organization of the means implicit in the cultural and social setting of the period. To be sure, there are numerous opportunities for expression and research in all fields but among them only a few which are positively related and favored by the dynamic forces of the age. In intuitively choosing certain esthetic or technical problems, the most sensitive and advanced artist is a tool for the recording of the time-expressive contents. That is, form and structure denote definite trends. The work of the artist corresponds to the creative problems in other fields, complementing them in the structure of civilization of that particular period.

Art may press for the sociobiological solution of problems just as energetically as the social revolutionaries do through political action. The so-called "unpolitical" approach of art is a fallacy. Politics freed from graft, party connotations, or more transitory tactics, is mankind's method of realizing ideas for the welfare of the community. Such a "weltanschaung" is transformed by the arts into emotional form, and becomes retroactive in the realm of conscious existence. This suggests that not only the conscious but also the subconscious mind absorbs social ideas which are then expressed in the specific media of the arts. Otherwise any problem could be successfully solved only through intellectual or verbal discourse. The difficulty lies in mass participation. The masses are filled with a petit bourgeois ideology, the masculine superman ideal promoted by papers and radios, books and films — by the unofficial education which the people have been taught to enjoy in spite of lip service to casual revolutionary ideas. Once their sensitivity is killed, they are unable to receive the message of art whether contemporary or old.

The success theory of the profit economy pays a high premium to the anti-artist. Artists are considered effeminate who do not have the stamina to participate in competition. This is not only untrue, as are most clichés, but tragic since at present art is perhaps the only field where convention does not completely suppress sentiment and where the omnipotence of thought and the independence of emotion are kept relatively intact. To follow the divining rod of intuition and expressive desire may often act as a psychological lifesaver especially in periods of hidden and open suppression of independent thought. The phrase that "the artist represents the consciousness and memory of his time" is a good characterization of his function. No society can exist without expressing its ideas, and no culture and no ethics can survive without participation of the artist who cannot be bribed.

Art represents the uncensored statement of its author; this is one of its most positive characteristics. No-one but the painter, the author, the composer is the sole master of his performance. The simpler his medium and the less investment it involves, the easier it is to avoid possible censorship and to preserve the ways of genuinely free expression.

Through his sensitivity the artist becqmes the seismograph of events and movements pertaining to the future. He interprets the yet hazy path of coming developments by grasping the dynamics of the present and by freeing himself from the momentary motivations and transitory influences but [not] without evaluating their trends. He is interested only in the recording and communicating of his vision. This is what materializes in his art. He cannot misuse such a situation. To be a "fulltime" worker, a "professional", involves a moral responsibility. This is why the secured existence of the uncompromising and incorruptible artist is so important to society ... The silly myth that genius has to "suffer" is the sly excuse of a society which does not care for its productive members unless their work promises immediate technological or economic applications with calculable profit...

Each generation differs from the preceding one in the determination of its task. The task of this generation is to search for its roots. It must try to understand the significance of natural functions so that everyone may become aware of the essential purpose of living: the preservation and refinement of the biological nature of the individual within a harmonious social existence. The value of such an existence will be measured in terms of cooperation, social usefulness and personal happiness. This new life requires a new methodology for approaching problems; a social mechanism of production and a creative education ... To meet the manifold requirements of this age with a definite program of human values, there must come a new mentality and a new type of personality. The common denominator is the fundamental acknowledgment of human needs; the task is to recognise the moral obligation is satisfying these needs, and the aim is to produce for human need, not for profit.

"Cannon-Fodder Can Talk"
Statement by Pvt. Dennis Mora

Contrary to what the Pentagon believes, cannon-fodder can talk. It is saying that we are not fighting for "freedom" in South Vietnam, but supporting a Hitler-loving dictator. It is saying that it will not accept as a rationale for exterminating a whole people, theories of dominoes, Chinese "aggression". It further says that the only foreign power in Vietnam today is the United States and that the Vietcong is an indigenous force which has the support of most of the people and is in control of 80% of the country.

It is a war of genocide. A genocide which has at its disposal the technology of a military chamber of horrors from bomblets to napalm, gas and defoliants. The American people are victims of their war in a very real sense. Apart from the tragedy of losing American boys in a war we cannot win, the war is a colossal waste of resources which are urgently needed here at home. The hypocrisy of a war on poverty is clear. It is all guns and no butter. The war has created inflation and the chief sufferer is the working man. Corporate profits soar and union men are told to hold to 3.2 wage increases in the "national interest". Free lunch programs are cut by 80%. Are we now ready to accept, in the national interest of course, the malnutrition of our children in order to incinerate Vietnamese children? This is the price we must pay for military miracles.

Joint statement by the Ft. Hood Three

We are Pfc. James Johnson, Pvt. David Samas and Pvt. Dennis Mora, three soldiers formerly stationed at Fort Hood, Texas in the same company of the 142 Signal Battalion, 2nd Armored Division. We have received orders to report on the 13th of July at Oakland Army Terminal in California for final processing and shipping to Vietnam.

We have decided to take a stand against this war, which we consider immoral, illegal and unjust. We are initiating today, through our attorneys, an action in the courts to enjoin the secretary of Defense and the Secretary of the Army from sending us to Vietnam. We intend to report as ordered to the Oakland Army Terminal, but under no circumstances will we board ship for Vietnam. We are prepared to face Court Martial if necessary.

We represent in our backgrounds a cross section of the Army and of America. James Johnson is a Negro, David Samas is of Lithuanian and Italian parents, Dennis Mora is a Puerto Rican. We speak as American soldiers.

We have been in the army long enough to know that we are not the only G.I.'s who feel as we do. Large numbers of men in the service either do not understand this war or are against it.

When we entered the army, Vietnam was for us only a newspaper box score of G.I.'s and Viet Cong killed or wounded. We were all against it in one way or another, but we were willing to "go along with the program" believing that we would not be sent to Vietnam.

We were told from the very first day of our induction that we were headed for Vietnam. During basic training it was repeated often by sergeants and officers, and soon it became another meaningless threat that was used to make us take our training seriously.

But later Vietnam became a fact of life when some one you knew wondered how he could break the news to his girl, wife or family that he was being sent there. After he solved that problem, he had to find a reason that would satisfy him. The reasons were many — "Somebody's got to do it", "The pay is good", and "You've got to stop them some place" were phrases heard in the barracks and mess hall, and used by soldiers to encourage each other to accept the war as their own. Besides, what could be done about it anyway? Orders are orders.

As we saw more and more of this, the war became the one thing we talked about most and the one point we all agreed upon. No one wanted to go and more than that, there was no reason for anyone to go.

The Viet Cong obviously had the moral and physical support of most of the peasantry who were fighting for their independence. We were told that you couldn't tell them apart — that they looked like any other skinny peasant.

Our man or our men in Saigon has and have always been brutal dictators, since the Diem first violated the 1954 Geneva promise of free elections in 1956.

The Buddhist and military revolt in all the major cities proves that the people of the cities also want an end to Ky and U.S. support for him.

The Saigon Army has become the advisor to American G.I.'s who have to take over the fighting.

No-one used the word "winning" anymore because in Vietnam it has no meaning. Our officers just talk about five or ten more years with at least 1/2 million of our boys thrown into the grinder. We have been told that many times we face a Vietnamese woman or child and that we will have to kill them. We will never go there — to do that — for Ky!

We know that Puerto Ricans are being drafted and end up in the worst of the fighting all out of proportion to their numbers in the population and we have first hand knowledge that that these ar the ones who have been deprived of decent education and jobs at home.

The three of us, while stationed together, talked a lot and found that we thought alike on one over-riding issue — the war in Vietnam must be stopped. It was all talk and we had no intention of getting into trouble by making waves at that stage.

Once back in Texas we were told that we were on levy to Vietnam. All we had discussed and thought about now was real. It was time for us to quit talking and decide. Go to Vietnam and ignore the truth or stand and fight for what we know is right.

We have made our decision. We will not be a part of this unjust, immoral, and illegal war. We want no part of a war of extermination. We oppose the criminal waste of American lives and resources. We refuse to go to Vietnam !!!!!!

The "Ft. Hood Three" have been sentenced to three years (Mora) and five years (Johnson, Samas) at hard labor. Their fight must be carried on. The genocidal assault on Vietnam must be stopped. For further information on the "Ft. Hood Three" contact:

Fort Hood Three Defense Committee, 5 Beekman St., 10th Floor, New York, N.Y., 10038

BLACK MASK

No. 3   JAN. 1967   5 Cents

BLACK MASK NO. 3 - January 1967

The etching on the front page was taken from a series, "The Caprices", published in 1797 by the Spanish artist Francisco Goya

The "ASSES"

The frightening truth of Goya's observation is not only still with us, but its reality has spread. Now, with the development of the mass-media the "asses" are able to reach further and with greater effectiveness.

Those perennial "asses," government and religion, are still spreading their lies; while they burn people alive daily, they indict others for "inciting to riot"; while they stifle the mind, they speak of free expression; while they pray for peace, they wage war - but now they have been joined by others, and the ranks of the "asses" grow. Not least among these are the schools, which have become little more than propaganda mills and training grounds for a destructive, de-humanizing society. What is more disturbing than seeing 2,700 students (Harvard) apologize to Defense Secretary McNamara, who as a war criminal will soon go on trial before the world. The hope lies not with these "good" students, but with those who have either left school to join the revolution, or who are continuing to fight on the educational front, such as in Berkeley. The hope lies with these students whom the N.Y. Times calls "nihilists" (which they certainly are not) rather than with the "annihilators" sitting in the pentagon.

The following was received from S.N.C.C. and shows that more than "due process" is needed, even if the liberal "asses" and their coalition-socialist allies don't think so.

As a follow-up to the Nov. 8th elections in that state (Alabama), and as a result of black people voting in those elections for the first time in their lives, the white landowners are retaliating by evicting large masses of black farm workers from their land.

In Greene County, the Greene County Freedom Organization reports that there have been a series of evictions, resulting in 70 families being evicted from the land which has been their only home for years.

In Lowndes County, several families have already been evicted from their homes and are now living in tents. Many more expect eviction notices after the picking season is over. Besides the eviction there have been brutal attacks by Lowndes County whites on black people who participated in the Nov. 8th elections, one of the worst cases being the beating of Andrew Jones who was hospitalised with a skull fracture ...

Wall St. is "War" St.

The first action of Black Mask (Oct. 66) was the closing of the Museum of Modern Art. The museum was symbolic to us of the total suppression of man (by the alienation of creation from life) - but this was only one aspect of our planned assault - social, economic and cultural. The next target is Wall Street. Specifically Wall Street's war on Vietnam and its accompanying war on the American poor and working class through the cutbacks on needed funds and a 3.2% ceiling on workers demands, as well as the constant call for their son's blood to fill the battlefield of butchery. We are not abandoning the cultural front but rather showing the interrelatedness of the struggle.

Peace advocates are certainly (for the most part) well intentioned, but without an accompanying understanding of the profit of war and the economic needs which it satisfies, they cannot hope to see peace. A system based on internal and external exploitation is itself the enemy.

During the first week in February, twenty-five "Masked" men will march on Wall Street and change its name to War Street. The accompanying statement, prepared in cooperation with Dan Georgakas, brother and poet, will be handed out along the way, in an attempt to expose the connection.

WALL STREET IS WAR STREET

The traders in stocks and bones shriek for New Frontiers - but the coffins return to the Bronx and Harlem. Bull markets of murder deal in a stock exchange of death. Profits rise to the ticker tape of your dead sons. Poison gas RAINS on Vietnam. You cannot plead "WE DID NOT KNOW." Television brings the flaming villages into the safety of your home. You commit genocide in the name of freedom.

BUT YOU TOO ARE THE VICTIMS!

If unemployment rises, you are given work, murderous work. If education is inferior, you are taught to kill. If the blacks get restless, they are sent to die. This is Wall Street's formula for the great society!

Art and Revolution

We are neither artists, nor anti-artists. We are creative men - revolutionaries. As creative men we are dedicated to building a new society but we must also destroy the existing travesty. What art will replace the burned bodies and dead minds which this society is producing? How can we create (since creation is life) as life is being crushed. Yet we must. We must create the tools with which we will replace this horror. We must create the seeds of the new - both psychological and physical - not alone but in the ranks of the masses, neither leading them nor being led.

The false concept of art cannot contain us; what is needed is much more, a form that will embrace the totality of life. This false concept was not even satisfactory in the past. How many so-called artists were not accepted as such in their lifetime, only to be embraced later when man learned to widen his vision. The primitive cultures had no idea of art, but only the natural responses of man. Their creative impulses embraced both the spiritual and the physical - the idols and the tools - the unknown and the known - in fact, the totality of life itself. Obviously we can't go back even if we want to (which we don't) but we can go forward, and a civilization with the abundant resources such as ours, can and should reach a point where this totality is once again dominant on an even larger scale.

We have no desire to set up new rules to replace the old. We believe that man, once liberated, will sense his direction. A free man never returns to slavery on his own volition, but we must prevent his being returned there by outside forces, one weapon being education and free creativity. Different personalities, environments, ages will determine the forms men develop, each potentially as valuable a part of the totality as the other. A few examples should suffice as illustration.

The Russian Revolution along with its social changes, brought about a cultural upheaval. Many saw the death of easel-painting (as far as we are concerned it was always dead, those creative men who utilized it always sought more than it was thought to offer. Thus a Van Gogh differs from a Bougereau). We heralded the death of "art for art's sake," but this again was a false issue. Were the cave markings made as art. Did the Primitives produce for "art's sake", or the early

Christians, or pre and early Renaissance such as Giotto, or the other creative men all the way through to the 20th century, which burst with Futurism. What did happen in 1917, was the chance for the creative man to function within a social revolution. There were two main approaches, one represented by Malevitch and the other by Tatlin.

The theory of laboratory art, as developed by Malevitch, made use of the individualistic work of the creative man in both its psychological and physical potential, first by opening the mind's vision and second by laying the basis for an ordered arrangement of man's surroundings. The other approach, as represented by Tatlin, was to take the material needs and to then translate them into a creative entity. Since each arose out of the psychological needs of their founders and the social needs of a dawning society they were both a part of the revolution. It is only later when the bureaucracy and the then rising Stalinism forced a false movement, socialist-realism, upon the scene that creativity stopped.

The same years (1917-1925) did, in different places and with different individuals, see different answers. The war torn west with its bourgeois dominance could not be expected to follow the same course as a post-revolutionary Russia. Yet there were some similarities even here. The German Bauhaus took a constructivist attitude (sometimes joining the two) while the Dutch De Stijl, followed a course more similar to that of Malevitch. But here the Dadaists enter, with a totally different and just as important role. They were undermining an effete and moribund society, a society whose destruction would benefit all. They were, as revolutionaries, in the streets and as creative men they sought to overthrow that perverted civilization which wreaked havoc on the world. This same goal was later sought by the Surrealists, with their attempts at building a new psychological experiment, as well as an emphasis on direct revolution, to destroy the bourgeoisie rather than hoping to shock them into awareness (the latter had been somewhat prevalent in the Dadaist movement, excepting the Berlin branch).

Yet we are of a new age. We have learned from the past, but to hell with the past. One of these can be ours - we are not so lucky. There will be similarities but there will be differences. We have digested them all but only to reject them as fertilizer from which the new will rise on its own, in the natural process of growth. There are emerging forces; cybernation, growing weaponry, and world-wide revolution which we are affected by and which we in turn must affect. We can and must re-shape the total environment; physical and psychological, social and aesthetic, leaving no boundaries to divide man. The future is ours, but not without a struggle.

B.M.

Todays authentic art goes hand in hand with revolutionary social activity: like the latter it leads to the confusion and destruction of capitalist society.

It is they [the young] who will mold the future, they will solve the problems we have not solved.

André Breton

Bertrand Russell: U.S. war crimes

I appeal to you, citizens of America, as a person concerned with liberty and social justice. Many of you will feel that your country has served these ideals and, indeed, the United States possesses a revolutionary tradition which in its origins, was true to the struggle for human liberty and for social equality. It is this tradition which has been traduced by the few who rule the U.S. today. Many of you may not be fully aware of the extent to which your country is controlled by industrialists who depend for their power partly on great economic holdings in all parts of the world. The U.S. today controls over 60% of the world's natural resources although it contains only 6% of the world's population. The minerals and produce of vast areas of the planet are possessed by a handful of men. I ask you to consider the words of your own leaders, who sometimes reveal the exploitation they have practiced.

The New York Times of Feb.12, 1950, said:"Indo-China is a prize worth a large gamble. In the North are exportable tin, tungsten, manganese, coal, lumber & rice; rubber, tea, pepper & hides. Even before World War II Indo-China yielded dividends estimated at $300 million per year."

One year later, an adviser to the U.S. State Department said the following; "We have only partially exploited Southeast Asia's resources. Nevertheless, Southeast Asia supplied 90% of the world's crude rubber, 60% of its tin and 80% of its copra and coconut oil. It has sizeable quantities of sugar, coffee, tobacco, sisal, fruits, tea spices, natural resins and gums, iron, petroleum, oil and bauxite."

And in 1953, while the French were still in Vietnam fighting with American backing, President Eisenhower stated: "Now let us assume we lost Indo-China. If Indo-China goes, the tin and tungsten we so greatly value would cease coming. We are after the cheapest way to prevent something terrible — the loss of our ability to get what we want from the riches of the Indo-China territory and from Southeast Asia."

This makes clear that the war in Vietnam is a war like that waged by the Germans in East Europe. It is a war designed to protect the continued control over the wealth of the region by American capitalists. When we consider that the fantastic sums of money spent on armament are awarded in contracts to the industries on whose boards of directors sit the generals who demand the weapons, we can see that the military and the large industry have formed an interlocking alliance for their own profit.

I appeal to you to consider what has been done to the people of Vietnam by the U.S. government. Can you, in your hearts, justify the use of poison chemicals and gas, the saturation bombing of the entire country with jelly-gasoline and phosphorus? Although the American press lies about this, the documentary evidence concerning the nature of these gases and chemicals is overwhelming.

They are poisonous and they are fatal. Napalm and phosphorus burn until the victim is reduced to a bubbling mass. The U.S. has also used weapons like the Lazy Dog, which is bomb containing 10,000 million slivers of razor-sharp steel. The razor darts slice to ribbons the villagers upon whom these weapons of sheer evil are constantly used. In one province of North Vietnam, the most densely populated, 100 million slivers of razor sharp steel have fallen in a period of 13 months.

In violation of solemn international agreements signed by American presidents and ratified by the American Congress, this Johnson has committed war crimes, crimes against humanity and crimes against peace. It has committed these crimes because the Johnson government exists to preserve the economic exploitation and the military domination of subject people by the U.S. industrial magnates and their military arm. The Central Intelligence Agency, which has a budget 15 times larger than all the diplomatic activity of the U.S., is involved in the assassination of heads of state and plots against independent governments. This sinister activity is designed to destroy the leadership and organization of peoples who are struggling to free themselves from the stranglehold of American economic and political domination. U.S. militarism is inseparable from the same predatory capitalism which reduced the American people themselves to poverty within the living memory of this generation. The same essential motives have led to barbarous and atrocious crimes on a great scale in Vietnam.

I have called on intellectuals and eminent independent men and women from all parts of the world to join in an international War Crimes Trribunal which will hear evidence concerning the crimes of the U.S. government in Vietnam. You will remember that the Germans were considered guilty if they acquiesced in and accepted the crimes of their government. Nobody considered it sufficient excuse for Germans to say that they knew about the gas chambers and the concentration camps, the torture and the mutilation, but were unable to stop it. I appeal to you as a human being to human beings. Remember your humanity and your own self respect. The war against the people of Vietnam is barbaric. It is an agressive war of conquest. It is Americans who have been killing Vietnamese, attacking villages, occupying cities, using gas and chemicals, bombing their schools and hospitals — all this to protect the profits of American capitalism. The men who conscript the soldiers are the same men who sign the military contracts in their own benefit. They are the same men who send American soldiers to Vietnam as company cops, protecting stolen wealth.

(The full text from which the above was excerpted was originally printed in the National Guardian. For further information on the War-Crimes Tribunal contact The Bertrand Russell Peace Foundation N.Y. office, 342 West 84th St., N.Y., N.Y. 10024)

BLACK MASK

No. 4   FEB - MAR   1967   5 Cents

Photo: Laurence B. Fink

BLACK MASK

BLACK MASK No. 4 - February-March 1967

Revolution: Now and Forever

We have marched on Wall Street (Feb. 10). We have changed its name to War Street. Wall Street remains and the war goes on. But we are not powerless, this monster can be stopped. First we must expose the enemy, speak it's name to the world - "War" St. Yet we can't stop there, for beyond Capitalism lies the whole rotten civilization known as the western world. A civilization rotten to its core.

We are not the first to say this, nor are we the only ones saying it now. The text reproduced below was taken from a Surrealist manifesto, "Revolution Now and Forever" issued in 1925.

> "Wherever western civilization is dominant all human contact has disappeared, apart from contact out of which money can be made - strictly cash payment. For over a century, human dignity has been reduced to the rank of an exchange value. It is already unfair; it is monstrous that a man who owns nothing should be enslaved by a man who owns property, but when this oppression exceeds salaried labor and assumes, for instance, the form of slavery which international high finance imposes upon whole populations, it is an iniquity which no massacre will ever succeed in expiating(...)

> It is our rejection of all accepted law, our hope in new, subterranean forces, capable of overthrowing history, which makes us turn our eyes towards Asia (today read as the third-world).

Categorically we need freedom, but a freedom based on our deepest spiritual needs and on the most human desires of our bodies. The time is up for the contemporary world. The stereotyped gestures, acts and lies of Europe have gone through their whole dirty circle. Spinoza, Kant, Blake, Hegel, Schelling, Proudhon, Marx, Stirner, Baudelaire, Lautreamont, Nietzsche: this list alone is the beginning of your downfall. It is the turn of the mongols to Bivouac in our squares. We should never for a moment worry that this violence could take us by surprise or get out of hand. As far as we are concerned, it could never be enough, whatever happens. All that should be seen in our behaviour is the absolute confidence which we have in a sentiment common to all of us, the sentiment of revolt, on which anything of any value is based. We are the revolt of the spirit. We believe that sanguinary revolution is the inevitable vengeance of a spirit humiliated by your doings. We are not utopian; we can conceive this revolution only in a social form. If anywhere there are men who have seen a coalition form against them, then they should never forget that revolution is the best and most effective safeguard of the individual."

Yes, Revolution. A revolution whose scope is as wide as the cosmos (from telescope to microscope), whose power is as strong as the millions who inhabit the third-world or the rockets which pierce the outer-world. A revolution which will destroy the exploitative traditions of the west including those noxious philosophies, liberalism and humanism, in whose name the world has been laid open to plunder.

Cardinal Spellman says, "The war in Vietnam is a war for civilization." We say, the civilization which wages a war like that in Vietnam, cannot be destroyed soon enough. We do not deny its accomplishments, but rather claim they arose in spite of this civilization, not because of it. When all men are free these accomplishments will be multiplied by the thousands: then we will have atomic energy to warm man not to burn him; machines to aid man not to cripple him.

We are now in an era which can do the most for man - or the most against him. We know what this civilization would do. Now we must decide what we will do.

The New Establishment

The following letter was sent to the "East Village Other" several weeks ago by the Black Mask group.

"Dear Editor: The Leary article "You Are a God Act Like One," in the last E.V.O. is one of the best examples of double speak we have yet seen - 1984 must be getting near.

No, Leary, we are not "Gods" we are flesh and blood men. Men like those whose lives are being crushed by this system you try so hard to protect. "No

From: George Bennett, Public Relations
Time: Wednesday, August 29, at 10 A.M.
Place: Hotel Astor, Yacht Room, 8th Flr.
Occasion: "Miss Mississippi" visits New
York en route to Miss America
contest; Stops at Hotel Astor

Beautiful Charlotte Ann Carroll, "Miss Mississippi of 1962," will say "hello" to New York tomorrow morning,Wednesday, Aug. 29, at 10 a.m. in the Yacht Room on the 8th floor of the Hotel Astor, where she is stopping during her visit to our city. The southern beauty is on her way to the "Miss America" Pageant.

"Miss Mississippi" has dark blonde curl hair and blue eyes, is 5' 8" tall, and measures 37-24-37. She will wear practice shorts for the photographers.

Miss Carroll is 19 years old and a sophomore studying education at Delta State College in Cleveland, Mississippi. She is an honor graduate of Europa (Miss.) High School, one of four daughters, and resides in Walthall, Mississippi, with her father, a grocer-farmer, and her mother, a city cl and Gallup poll taker.

An excellent horsewoman, Miss Carroll i part owner of a horse. She also swims, di water skis, sketches, sings, dances and wa three times named an All-State basketball champion while in high school.

Miss Carroll was also Webster County Fo estry Queen. She was chosen "Miss Mississi over 47 southern beauties on the basis of suit and talent competitions. Her "Olive O song-and-dance skit got one of the biggest ovations in the history of the Mississippi pageant.

abrupt destructive, rebellious actions, please." The Luce Publications know a good thing when they see it. If enough of them (Watts, Santo Domingo, Vietnam) "Drop-Out" we won't have to wipe them out. But they won't "Drop-Out" - instead they will drive you out - you power hungry politicians, you corrupted poets, you Madison Avenue Gods.

What is "The most practical, liberating message" that prophet Leary brings us? "Your state of consciousness is reflected in your environment. You create your environment." No, Leary, we don't create our environment, it has been created for us by those perverted creatures of government and business. But we will create a new one; one built on the ashes of the old, one where man doesn't have to be a "God" (or priest) to enjoy the fruits of this world, one where all men will be "Tuned-In" - Tuned in to life in all its glory. "No destructive, rebellious actions" - How else? Everyone in Harlem can "Turn-On" but Harlem won't change. Everyone in India can "Turn-On" but hunger won't vanish. Maybe you can "Turn-On" Leary and forget it, but we can't - but then we aren't Gods.

This letter is not meant as a criticism of drugs in general but of Leary in particular. Drugs are and should be a personal matter for the individual to decide (not cops and courts) but Leary is another matter. His advocacy of religion and his attempts to de-fuse, not spread, rebellion make him the enemy along with the cops and courts. Needless to say, the letter was not printed and Leary still inhabits Mt. Olympus while the E.V.O. serves as oracle for the "New Establishment."

This new establishment has all the mind sapping and anti-revolutionary characteristics of the old, with religion playing a dominant role: besides Leary, we have Allen Ginsberg acting as salesman for both Hinduism and Buddhism (this represents no conflict since sectarian theology is not the object, any religion will do, as long as it prevents revolution); and the press follows close behind. The most dangerous aspect of this establishment is the "radical" mantle with which it seeks to cover itself and thus delude many dissatisfied youth with a false bourgeois sponsored "rebellion." The artists speak against the war for one week, but serve the capitalists all year. The poets clamor at the gates of the university while the real poets are in the streets crying "Burn, Baby, Burn." And the East Village Other speaks of Anarchism but sells the reactionary line.

As Anarchists we feel particularly disturbed by this last distortion, the nature of which can be shown by one recent example. In his preface to "Interview With an Anarchist" (a so-called Anarchist who sees revolution as "almost impossible" so suggests mutilating I.B.M. cards and jamming parking meters: What an easy cop-out for the bourgeois renegade who realizes his inherent interest in preserving this system) the editor states, "The U.S.A. is a democracy founded on the proposition that all men are created equal and have the inalienable right to control their own destiny. A principle of anarchy is inherent in our government in that every four years, the opportunity presents itself to overthrow the administration by non-violent means of free elections." Bullshit, America is a non-democracy which places property rights above human rights. "Anarchy" is inherent in government but "Anarchism" opposes all government. We don't overthrow the administration every four years but rather change jailers and there are no free elections when a few men control the wealth (be it the capitalists of the west or the state-bureaucrats of the east). Revolution!

B. M.

Poetry Comes Out of the Barrel of a Gun

The weakwilled and weakminded love to live in calm and beauty without participating in struggle. Their favorite scene is peaceful existence behind the violence of a strong military and police force which they piously decry (with words) but never oppose (with deeds). They seek to reconcile irreconcilables in order to prevent hostility. They are ashamed to go to the Right and they are afraid to go to the Left. They escape to obscure vapors of mysticism and charming bowers of estheticism. They raid India for the sick religion which has maligned life on the subcontinent. Their estheticism assumes the chameleon form of anti-art and the-end-of-art-as-we-know-it proclaimed in ever multiplying incestuous publications/billboards/events/happenings et. nauseam. Their solution to an increasingly ugly world is to call one another "beautiful". False distinctions are drawn between inner/outer space. Anti-thought is cloaked with the bullshit phrase: we have come to the end of politics. The unity of opposites explicated by masters as varied as Lao and Marx is heralded as some new enlightenment but anyone whose LOVE has driven him to declare war on the enemy and to express his Hate forthrightly is regarded as some monster spawned in a Union Square sewer. The taste-makers declare this a season of costumes, amplified noise, intellectualized comic books and all freak outs extraordinary. But the sad truth is that most avant [garde] cinema is boring and that the generation under 25 has very little to teach and a great deal to learn. Pop art and its siblings are little more than apotheosis of capitalist reality. Even the revolt vs. Viet Genocide too often becomes yet another career building gimmick. Rather than posing a threat to the status quo, hippy culture furnishes whole new industries with vast empires of unexpected profits. Capitalist promoters have showblitzed the Underground into a perversion of rebellion which is not even a reasonable facsimile. The pursuit of the perpetual High is nothing more than the velvet down on the inside of the imperialist iron glove. While sweet lovey-dovies chant hare krishna in Manhattan parks, the kids of Asia are napalmed. The vast conspiracy for global crime tools up for its greatest atrocities and "rebels" protest with yellow chrysanthemums and paper submarines. The bells now tolling are not for guru Malcolm but for the system which assassinated him. Creative man undertakes the poetry of the deed or he flounders with the death strivers and suicides of this sad demented nation. Creative man does not entertain or shock the bourgeoisie. He destroys them!

Dan Georgakas

BLACK MASK

No. 5   APRIL   1967   5 Cents

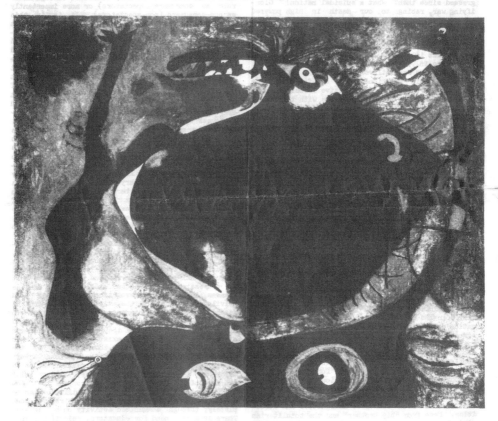

... the normally constituted bourgeoisie possesses rather less imagination than a worm and has, in place of a heart, a larger-than-life-sized
corn which only troubles him when there is a change in the weather--the
stock-exchange weather.

H. Arp (dada 1916-1920)

BLACK MASK No. 5 - April 1967

... the normally constituted bourgeoisie possesses rather less imagination than a worm and has, in place of a heart, a larger-than-life-sized corn which only troubles him when there is a change in the weather — the stock exchange weather.

H. Arp (dada 1916-1920)

The Wall St. stock holder needs no analyst. He knows only too well he has his money and nothing more. The market fell in '29, and this "leading" citizen began leaping from windows. Have we progressed since then? What a suicidal nation! Glorifying war, racing to our death in high powered automobiles, gorging ourselves with drugs, smoke and drink, while we anticipate death by purchasing burial sites, and life insurance. The case is simple. Poets have told us for too many years exactly what is needed... a soul... love... something to believe in... a spirit...

Governments are failures. Cultural as well as social-economic solutions must be found - those that take us back to our creative forces and away from destruction. The hope does lie with the young, but has our mechanized culture forced too many to simply reflect the aspirations of their forerunners? Where are the thousands, the millions, with the spirit of the students at Berkeley and of the youth in Watts? Where are the rebels, not the hippies? Where are the students who tolerate no more the drone of professors who cry for freedom of the mind as they realizing that life must be played in its totality that they will become unable to accept anything less, bringing them closer to those "with nothing to lose, but a world to gain" and therefore closer to revolution. The recent proposals that student activists, upon graduation, enter the "professional" community and seek to radicalize it from within is at least [self] defeating and at worst anti-revolutionary. One must realize that the professional, liberal and middle classes are, as classes, incapable of revolution since they hold privileged positions in the existing society and are dependent upon its continuation. This is not to suggest that students abandon their skills and training, but rather that they withdraw them from a system which in order to exist must prevent their full realization and place them instead at the service of humanity and revolution. But here we must emphatically reject the concept of revolution as a surrender to political machinations, while resuming the role of spectator, and instead oppose it with the concept of revolution as the ability of man to control and effect his life and environment completely, through communized activity on all levels. There is a real need for educators, scientists, artists, etc. but this need can only be fulfilled by their demands for full participation in the social fabric not by their acceptance of the limited role imposed from above. The true scientist, artist, etc. becomes revolutionary through the uncompromising pursuit of his work at the expense of a "career" and often his life (a case in point would be Wilhelm Reich, who realizing his role as scientist was not separable from that of the social revolutionary found himself constantly at odds with authoritarian society and having fled Nazi Germany, eventually died in an American prison).

B. M.

the world wide revolt of youth

In Strasbourg, France a group of "students" have attempted a study of the new forms of revolutionary activity being manifested by youth. The following excerpt is from a translation of their brochure made by participants in the Strasbourg action which included the liquidation of the official bureaucratic "student union".

After a long period of lethargic sleep and permanent counter-revolution a new contestation has been taking form for some years. Youth seems to be the carrier ... In reality this revolt of youth against an imposed way of life is only the advanced sign of a vaster subversion which will englobe all who suffer more and more under the impossibility of living. It is the prelude to the next revolutionary epoch. Only the dominant ideology and its daily organs (utilizing the proven mechanism of the inversion of reality) can reduce this real historic movement to a pseudo-category: The Idea of Youth — of which it is the essence to be revolted. Thus a new youth in revolt is recuperated by the notion of the eternal revolt of youth which reappears each generation and which naturally looses impetus as "the young man is taken into the seriousness of production". The "revolt of youth" has been and still is the object of a genuine inflation of journalism which makes this revolt a "spectacle" to be contemplated in order to prevent it from being lived. It is an accepted deviation

— already integrated, necessary for the continued functioning of the social system. This revolt against society actually reassures society since it is supposed to last only a short part of life and remain confined within the apartheid of "youth problems" — as there is a female "problem" or a negro "problem". [They are viewed as "problems" calling for reform instead of as social crisis demanding revolutionary change. So the "negro question" becomes one of "civil rights" rather than, as Malcolm X demanded, "Human Rights". One of ending "injustice" rather than ending the system which creates "injustice" ...ED] In reality, if there is "youth problem" it is only that the profound crisis of society is felt with more acuteness by youth and what ought to surprise us is not that the youth have revolted but that the adults are so resigned.

In the most concise way the "Blousons Noir" (Teddy boys, youth gangs) in every country express with violence their refusal to be integrated. Yet the abstract character of this refusal offers them no means to escape the contradictions of a system of which they are the spontaneous negative product.

The Provos constitute the first attempt to go beyond the experience of the "Blousons Noir", the organization of its first political expression. They were born thanks to the encounter between some dregs of decomposed art in search of success and a mass of revolted youth in search of affirmation. Since the formation of their organization the two tendencies have remained distinct: the mass without theory found itself straight away under the tutelage of a thin layer of suspect leaders who tried to maintain their "power" by the secretion of a "provotarian" ideology ... Whereas the need is no less than an uninterrupted revolution to change life, the Provo hierarchy believes (as Bernstein believed to transform capitalism into socialism by reforms) that it is enough to provide some improvements in order to modify everyday life. The Provos in choosing the fragmentary end by accepting the totality ...Having lost hope of transforming the totality, they lose hope in those forces which alone hold the means of possible transcendence. The proletariat is the motor of capitalist society and therefore its mortal danger: everything is done to repress it (political parties, bureaucratic syndicates, police, more often than against the Provos, the colonization of his whole life) for here is the one really menacing force. [In America this would be the blacks, Puerto Ricans, Mexicans, poor whites and unskilled laborers rather than the higher paid "workers", though automation and the growth of wild-cat strikes will radicalize many of these. Yet we must not forget that government still found it necessary to jail James Hoffa — as an attack on organized labor ...ED] The Provos have understood nothing of this; unable to criticize the system of production they remain prisoners of the whole system. When during an anti-syndicalist workers riot their base rallied to direct violence, the leaders were completely overtaken by the movement and in their bewilderment found nothing better than to denounce this "excess" and to call them back to pacifism, dismally renouncing their program of provoking authority, in order to show its repressive character, and crying that they were provoked by the police. The revolted base of the Provos can come to a revolutionary criticism only by rejecting these leaders and beginning to rally the objective forces of the proletariat ... There only can the Provos rejoin the real contestation which already has a base among them. If they truly want to transform the world, they have only to paint in white those who seek to content themselves.

"Hell No"

Native American Appeal

This can be considered as an Indian appeal to all minority groups within America — as well as to those whites still possessing a moral conscience or code — to form a coalition movement dedicated to righting the wrongs within American society itself before embarking upon the self-appointed role of world policeman ...

The Indian's objective today is stated simply enough, to regain every single acre of land that they can, and to receive proper indemnity for all they cannot regain. All of this in order that they may lay the economic foundations for rebuilding an Indian way of life. To bring to an end, finally the intolerable conditions under which they live today, conditions which give them a life expectancy of 43 years. Is there a racial crime worse than the theft of life itself? No other group of people in American society has a life expectancy as low as the Indian. And the time has come to put an end, once and for all, to the cruel farce of attempting to integrate him into a society for which he is not adapted, historically or culturally ...

The negro aims at nothing less than full integration into American society. He is now fighting to have his children bussed to predominantly white schools, for his right to live in predominantly white residential district, for his full share of jobs at all levels, for his civil rights, in short for an end to every single form of racial discrimination against him in America. And he has every right to these objectives, if that is what he really wants.

But this is not the Indian's goals. [nor is it the black man's — see article following.] He is fighting desperately to retain his identity not to lose it. He doesn't want his children bussed to predominantly white schools, he doesn't want to live in a white neighbourhood ...

No, the Indian wants his own way of life, and who is to say that he is wrong? To obtain this goal he must have his broken treaties reviewed by international tribunal in which other colored nations have representation and whose decision is final. To gain these ends he must join in a coalition with the other minority groups in America, helping them to gain redress for their grievances in exchange for aid in his own fight. They might adopt as their slogan the old saying — "an injury to one is an injury to all".

The Survival of American Indians Assoc.

P.O.Box 719, Tacoma, Washington

Afro-American, Puerto Rican Unity

The question of cultural identity is a very important matter to Afro-Americans, because it has been consistently denied us. Society tells us in many ways that to be successful, to be intelligent, to be beautiful, one cannot be black. For example when people in the U.S. talk about integration it is always in terms of black children being able to go to a white school, black parents being able to move into a white neighbourhood. This amounts to saying that nothing black — nothing of our own — can be good. The society teaches our people to try and be white as possible, and so they are ashamed of their features — they try to straighten their hair. Throughout the country, but especially in the south, black people are denied knowledge of their history and culture; They are taught that they are worthless. In a similar way, Puerto Ricans who come to the U.S. also experience pressure to accept the values of the dominant society in order to be successful.

Black Power means for us liberation from oppression by the racist white power structure of the U.S. It means that we will control our own Afro-American communities. That we will direct our affairs. That we will have power in the political and economic arenas ...

But our vision is not merely of a society in which black men have power to rule the lives of other black men. The society we seek to build among black people is not an oppressive capitalistic society. It is a society in which the spirit of community and humanistic love will prevail. We do not want merely to see black money go into black pockets; we want it to go into the communal pocket. We want to see the cooperative concept applied in business and banking and housing. In schools we want the community to decide how the schools should be run — not a group of administrators who do not understand the problems of the community.

We seek, therefore to change the power bases of the world. The powerless should now begin to have power. This is one reason why we refuse to fight in the American army against the Vietnamese people. The American army takes advantage of the Afro-American masses. It uses them to fight our own brothers. It tells us that we are going to fight for a so-called "Democracy" but we know the hypocrisy of that claim. We know in our flesh and in our blood, what American democracy means. For this reason we are absolutely — I repeat absolutely — opposed to the drafting of young people of any nationality who are oppressed like us. If we are to fight we will fight — but in our own country, to liberate our people. We have only one answer to the draft: Hell No!

We who stand with the poor of the earth, must unite. Brothers of Puerto Rico let us unite to achieve our goals. The forces of oppression, although very powerful are only a minority compared to the power which all the oppressed of the world can wield. We should remember these words: The poor shall never be crushed because they are too close to the earth.

From a speech by Stokely Carmichael — Univ. of Puerto Rico, January 25, 1967.

BLACK MASK

No. 6   MAY- JUNE   1967   5 Cents

BLACK MASK No. 6 - May/June 1967

Photos: Karl Bermann

"Hell No! Blacks won't go!" Waiting in Central Park for the April 15 Mobilization farce to get underway, the Harlem contingent is spotted making their way down Central Park West. They would not take the legal parade route, but would march down Seventh Avenue instead, minus police, barricades, or parade permit. Screams from the park - "We're joining them!" Thousands of people break the parade line and begin running out of the park - jumping benches, fences, knocking over pedestrians. The militant spirit of the blacks has caught on!

Down Fifty-ninth Street, revolutionary banners, NLF flags, black flags. The crowd of eight to ten thousand breaks into a mad stampede - they realize they have the streets! (the peaceniks and bourgeoisie wait impotently in Central Park, unaware of those who have broken the line).

Twenty-five abreast move down Seventh Avenue. Traffic is paralyzed for blocks - pedestrians stare dumbfounded. Police have no idea what is happening. The blacks in front, the revolutionary contingent, anarchists and some not even aware that they have broken away from the mildness and futility of "demonstrations." This is no longer a "demonstration." These people have joined with the Zengakuren of Japan, the students of Spain and Latin America. Revolution! Not reformism.

"Hell no! We ain't going!" - "How many kids did you kill today" into Times Square. All hell has broken lose! Twenty-odd blocks now filled with people. Revolutionary banners surround the Times Sq. recruiting station - a surreal sight indeed! Led by the revolutionary contingent, the crowd surges up Forty-second

Street (the Harlem group had already turned into Forty-sixth Street enroute to the U.N.). Fearful drivers roll up their windows. Traffic is halted on the busiest street in the city!

Approaching First Avenue, the police! Suddenly, those in the front line are clubbed - in the middle they are surrounded and practically crushed by a human chain of police. In a group the marchers had remained powerful. Yet, unprepared for the police and their brutal methods they were easily divided and quelled.

This action was never reported in the New York dailies - but it did happen and it must happen again and again!

Janice Morea

The April 15 Mass Mobilization which saw at least 300,000 people march to the U.N. has come and gone. The war remains! The preceding account of the 'break-away" march - which was exactly that, physically and psychologically, first by leaving the line of march and its prescribed route and second by leaving the concept of "symbolic" protest, with its incumbent belief in moral persuasiveness, for the road of direct action - and the following article on "resistance" point out the two most important directions. Neither excludes the other, while both contribute to a singular end - not of war - but of that which produces war. But more importantly the idea of resistance, based on social and economic struggle must also form the basis for the first, otherwise it too will remain "protest" though of a more radical nature.

"RESIST"

A comment on the Spring Mobilization to End the War in Vietnam Now, reprinted from "The New Orleans Movement for a Democratic Society" newsletter.

Our readers will recall in our last newsletter that we commented on the "Spring Mobilization" by stating our refusal to support it.

We pointed out that (1) demonstrations in New York and San Francisco, long the traditional centers of political activity, would do nothing to build the necessary long-term movement based on a perspective of struggle with the Government and consisting of those oppressed classes with the power and motivation to establish political and economic democracy; and (2) the whole undemocratic way in which the demonstration and the coalition behind it was put together made it unacceptable to anyone desiring to build a movement controlled by its members rather than a few "leaders......"

Consider the 1963 March on Washington for Freedom and Jobs. Was anybody liberated? Did anyone (except the organizers of the march) get a job? Racism, we learned, was a major part of the U.S. economic and political system. You did not end racism by going to Washington and begging the Government to stop oppressing black people. Victories over racism are won by black people when and only when they organize themselves for political and economic power.

The U.S. Government has been involved in aggression against the people of Vietnam, North and South, for 13 years - or 20 years if you include U.S. support for French imperialism. The war in Vietnam is not a mistake; it is the result of a carefully conceived if not always completely successful plan to preserve and expand U.S. economic enslavement of South East Asia. No demonstration no matter how "broad" and "responsible" is going to convince the U.S. Government and the big corporations to give up South East Asia! It should be abundantly clear to the southern movement that we too can only score victories over the Government's foreign and domestic policies of oppression and violence when we organize ourselves to win political and economic power....

Are we brothers to the Vietnamese people, struggling alongside them against a common enemy which oppresses us both? Or, are we merely appalled at the naked brutality of genocidal war and wish our rulers would come up with a more sophisticated way of keeping these "uppity gooks" in their place? The main thrust of the "Spring Mobilization" stuff that we've seen indicates that, for them, the main question is war or peace. And they're for peace.

The Vietnamese feel somewhat differently about the matter. They are for their liberation first and peace second. They will not live in the barbarous "peace" of U.S. imperialism. They would rather die free than live as slaves... For the Vietnamese, the liberation of their country from foreign occupation and domestic tyranny is not negotiable. We and many people agree. But we think this not only holds true for Vietnam but for our own country as well. We will struggle to build a movement of "struggle," we will fight to build a fighting and winning movement. Since no tyranny concedes anything without political and economic power being brought to bear against it, we intend to build a movement that will force the power structure to concede all of its power to the people.

We are not and will not become the "loyal opposition." We are not loyal to U.S. imperialism. Our loyalties are to the American people and their liberation. The Vietnamese and all the world's oppressed and struggling peoples are our brothers, their enemy is also ours.

I suspect this is where the lines will be drawn; when the current chaos in the left settles down a bit, we will clearly see on one side those who do not feel themselves oppressed in this country and hence do not look at things from the view of the oppressed here and in Vietnam, and on the other side those who are oppressed and ready to unite with all other oppressed peoples. We hope and believe our brother southern movement will make their choice and follow the example of the heroic vietnamese people: Better to fight for liberation than live in peace as a slave.

When we resist, we will win.

Ed Clark

Revolution or National Liberation?

Our support for the Vietnamese people is unequivocal. This is no "war," but an act of naked aggression by a major power seeking to conquer a small, relatively backward nation (technologically not culturally) for economic and political reasons. To speak of negotiations is criminal; even to call for immediate unconditional withdrawal of all American personnel, military and non-military, is insufficient since the the world is full of potential Vietnams where they can be transferred, but rather we must seek to end the source of this barbarism - American capitalism. But is that enough? Has capitalism been the first or last form of tyranny over man (though it is unquestionably the most active today)? We think not! Therefore the call for its defeat both internally and externally must be accompanied by that which we hope to replace it. Not "National Liberation" but "Total Revolution."

The irony is that Vietnam, which is waging a "War of Liberation" (south) and one of defense against assault (north) is closer in many ways to what we seek, due to the nature of their struggle, than anywhere else. The north under the reality of American bombs has been forced to de-centralize, placing control of production in many areas into the hands of the local population with a minimum of interference from Hanoi, while in the south the "liberated" areas have been left under the control of the inhabitants with an almost complete lack of bureaucracy. But this is only because of the exigencies of war and the existence of a singular will to defeat the common enemy. We are sure this situation will change, for once the war is concluded, assuming the Americans have been prevented from carrying out the total destruction of Vietnam (north and south) the natural function of government to suppress (to govern) the masses will reassert itself. Once the war is over, the masses must struggle to retain complete control of the land and means of production for the needed task of rebuilding , not the "Socialist State," but rather the communist (libertarian) society. Not "National Liberation," which though freeing Vietnam from foreign domination leaves the economy under the control of the managers and the bureaucrats but "Revolution" with its own institutions of self-management, workers councils and communes. Not "National Liberation" but "total, world wide revolution."

B. M.

The "Klefts:" Warrior-poets

Byron and Shelley were kleftic poets. And Mayakovsky. And De Sade. Brothers of the Greek brigands who choose the freedom of the peaks over bondage to the Turkish Bey. From their mountain strongholds the klefts raided the rich, the quislings, and the oppressor himself. A share of the booty went to the villagers who soon understood the klefts (thieves) were their own true soul. And at night around their fires the klefts danced and made up poems to sing to one another. And in the valleys the young men heard them, and one by one, the bravest made their way to the mountain tops. For the dances and courage and poetry of the klefts were the essence of liberation. Like Baudelaire at the barricades of the Commune. Like Lorca. Because Lumumba too was a poet. And Sitting Bull performed the Sun Dance before the Custer fight. As Le Roi Jones and Watts guerrillas create kleftic cantos. As even in the poisonous cauldron of white America, the kleftic strain rises to war against Establishment and Spectacle. The warrior poet takes up his santouri and his weapons and the Junta understands full well.

Dan Georgakas

Harlem Six

"Six young negro men, the eldest of whom is twenty, have lately been imprisoned by the State of N.Y. for life. The charge against them is murder. The charge is almost certainly false, but, in any case, it has not been proved. These young men are citizens of a country which has sworn to bring freedom to the Vietnamese; if they were not in prison, they would almost surely be in the Asian jungles, defending the morality of the Western World. But the morality to which they have been subjected cannot possibly be desired by the Vietnamese, nor by anyone who desires to live....

"I appeal to you, in the name of our common humanity, and for the sake of our common survival, to join me in protesting the outrages perpetrated against these men...." - James Baldwin.

For more information on the Harlem Six, or for copies of the petition by James Baldwin, from which the above is excerpted, contact the Charter Group, Box 245, Cathedral Station NYC 10025; funds needed for court appeals, etc.

And so we have the Harlem Six. Or is it 6,000 or 6,000,000; victims of racist violence. Whether "legal" or illegal it is all the same. James Powell, killed by an off duty cop (N.Y.). Leonard Deadwyler, killed by on duty cops (L.A.). Four dead - Harlem 1964. Thirty-four dead - Watts 1965 and how many thousands more. Genocide. And now the summer advances, with its talk of riots. But there are no riots, only the frustration, the anger, the rebellion of the oppressed. There are no riots, only the enraged violence of those, who are themselves victims of perpetual violence. Police brutality was only the spark - the brutality of life was the fuel. And this life has not changed. And the summer advances. So now we have plans for more brutality and more repression. And the blacks are blamed - "riots."

Chattel slavery was violence as wage-slavery is violence (property is violence!). But no, it is only the victims who are violent. So we make plans to mobilize the National Guard - violence. We strengthen the police force - violence. We invade the ghetto - violence. We crush discontent - violence. But no, it is only the victims who are violent. The City of Cleveland makes plans to destroy black youth - violence. The National Rifle Association calls for armed posses - violence. Atlanta readies armored vehicles - violence. But no, only the victims are violent.

And since the environment is maintained by violence, there is no alternative to the violence of the masses. "That is why we are revolutionaries and not because we are desperate men, thirsting for revenge and filled with hate." (Enrico Malatesta - 1922).

Editors

BLACK MASK

No. 7   AUGUST-SEPT.   1967   **5 Cents**

A new dynamism exists; one fueled by science and fired by revolution. One which has followed Futurism, Dadaism and Surrealism to a point where they must be left behind. Where they attempted to revolutionize "art" we must change life. We seek a form of action which transcends the separation between art and politics: it is the act of revolution.

Each culture determines those forms which its art will take and we seek nothing less than the destruction of this culture. We have an art which is a substitute for living, a culture which is an excuse for the utter poverty of life. The call for revolution can be no less than "total". To change the wielders of power is not enough, we must finally change life itself. Man must seize direct control of his environment—socially, economically and culturally. We can recognize no power outside of the people, no elite (whether it calls itself revolutionary or not) which determines the political direction, no separation between politics and the rest of life. The same must be done culturally—a "total" culture needs no experts, no artists—it needs only men.

BLACK MASK

No. 7   AUGUST-SEPT. 1967   **5 Cents**

BLACK MASK No. 7 - August/September 1967

A new dynamism exists; one fuelled by science and fired by revolution. One which has followed Futurism, Dadaism and Surrealism to a point where they must be left behind. Where they attempted to revolutionize "art" we must change life. We seek a form of action which transcends the separation between art and politics: it is the act of revolution.

Each culture determines those forms which its art will take and we seek nothing less than the destruction of this culture. We have an art which is a substitute for living, a culture which is an excuse for the utter poverty of life. The call for revolution can be no less than "total." To change the wielders of power is not enough, we must finally change life itself. Man must seize direct control of his environment - socially, economically and culturally. We can recognize no power outside of the people, no elite (whether it calls itself revolutionary or not) which determines the political direction, no separation between politics and the rest of life. The same must be done culturally - a "total" culture needs no experts, no artists - it needs only men.

All or Nothing

For too long we have witnessed the degeneration of revolutionary thought into an argument over method; as if the only question left open was "How" and not "What." It is time we questioned not only the means but also the content - thought as well as action: For together they are the revolution but separate they are a tragedy.

If the end is the taking of power by the people themselves then the means must be the revolutionary organs of the people - workers councils, community councils, communes, etc.

If the end is the freeing of man culturally as well as socially and economically then the means exist in the destruction of "culture."

If the end is the liberation of natural man then the means must be sexual as well as social.

If the end is the "totality" then the means must be "total" - all or nothing.

B. M.

At times, amidst the scenes of riot and destruction that made parts of the city look like a battlefield, there was an almost carnival atmosphere.

N.Y. Times 7/16/67.

Said Gov. Hughes after a motor tour of the riot-blighted streets...
"The thing that repelled me most was the holiday atmosphere... it's
like laughing at a funeral."

Time 7/21/67.

Yes! We laugh at this funeral. Poor frustrated wasp Hughes. Sure he cannot dig
the ultimate reason and human passion of what he calls "criminal" uprising. He
belongs to an obsolete generation, the last of a system at whose burial we cannot
but burst in joy. Esteeming the integrationist only so far as they integrate as house-
owner in this dying system; he is only repelled by their enjoyment, their holiday
atmosphere, as soon as they transcend the commodity enslavement and so do
transcend him. He is right, as he is stupid. Evidently the patriotic shit would not
stick to the Afro-American. Sure "they don't hate so much the white man as they
do hate America," America as it is abused and dominated by a handful of white,
clean washed, cool blooded gangsters. In their disgust of this America the Black
Man does not stay alone!

Tony

Revolution or its Abortion?

Revolution has failed and will fail as long as the state remains intact. Men in
revolutionary situations have been castrated by the bureaucratic apparatus of the
state and its institutions of control and coercion. False theories of organization
have led to the suppression of man's desire to construct his own life. Those who
recognize the miscarriage of the revolution know that the revolutionary project
must be radically transformed. General self-management, the conscious direction
by all of the whole of life can be its only goal as the revolutionary organization of
councils will be its adequate form. Collective as opposed to personal management
must reign.

In the brief history of the heights of proletarian struggles, the organization of
workers councils for workers management of production have been the moments
of revolutionary truth. Now there is a new proletariat composed of workers and
non-workers who have no power over their condition, the meaning and product of
their activities. In the struggle between the power and the new proletariat,
workers' and non-workers' councils will be the organs through which men rise to
resolve political, social and economic questions in function of their own lives. The
separation between these false categories, as the separation between work and
leisure time, will eventually be dissolved. Commodity production will be replaced
by production for life. Work itself will be attacked and transcended to be replaced
by a new type of free activity. The new proletariat will disappear when the
mainstays of commodity production - needless jobs, war, holds on automation,
positions in the bureaucracy - are destroyed. Councils may become the universal
form for this realization.

The fight against commodity production, against ideology (which is by necessity sectarian) in all its guises, against the State and the schism it imposes, will be led by workers' and community councils. Thus the role of councils will not be the self-management of the existing world, but its continual qualitative transformation. Man's total emancipation depends upon his ability to freely construct his life. The step from mere survival in a system to life must be made if the revolutionary project is to be worthwhile. Man's attempt to organize his own life must this time not be thwarted. Life, not survival - self-management, not subjugation must be the goal or there is no revolution.

Carol Verlaan

the Sexual Revolution
Wilhelm Reich
(1935,1944)

The social concepts of the 19th cent. with their purely economic definitions, no longer apply to the ideological stratification we see in the cultural struggles of the 20th cent. The social struggles of today, to reduce it to the simplest formula, are between the interests safeguarding and affirming life on the one hand, and the interests destroying and suppressing life on the other ...

If the basic social question is thus concretely formulated, then it goes without saying that what becomes the focus of social endeavor is the living functioning of every member of society ... In this connection the significance which, over 15 years ago, I ascribed to social sexual suppression, assumes gigantic proportions. Social and individual sex-economy has proved the suppression of infantile and adolescent sex life to be the basic mechanism by which character structures supporting political, ideological and economic serfdom are produced. It is no longer a matter of presenting a white, a yellow, a red or a black membership card to prove this or that mentality. It is a question of fully affirming, of aiding and safeguarding, the free and healthy life manifestations ... in an unmistakeable manner which forever excludes any social fraud — or of suppressing and ruining them, no matter with what ideology or alibi, whether "proletarian" or "capitalistic", for this or that religion, whether Jewish, Christian or Buddhist. This is true everywhere and as long as there is life, and must be recognized if one is to put an end to the organized defraudation of the masses of working individuals, if one wishes to prove in action that one takes one's democratic ideals seriously ...

The economic process, that is, the development of the machines, is functionally identical with the process of psychic structure in the people who create the economic process, who further or inhibit it and who are influenced by it. Economy without active human emotional structure is inconceivable; so is human feeling, thinking and acting without economic basis. Instead of talking so much about dialectics, one should try to comprehend the living mutual relationship between groups of people, nature and machines. They function as a unity, and at the same time mutually condition each other. Certainly, it will not be possible to master the present cultural process unless one comprehends the fact that the core of the psychic structure is the sexual structure, and that the cultural process is essentially determined by sexual needs.

The small, miserable, allegedly "unpolitical" sexual life must be studied in connection with the problems of authoritarian society. Politics does not take place at thediplomat's luncheon but in this everyday life. Social consciousness in everyday living, therefore is indispensable. If the millions of inhabitants of the world understood the activities of the leading hundred diplomats, everything would be all right. Then, society and human needs would no longer be governed according to armament interests and political exigency ...

The economic order of the past 200 years has changed the human structure considerably. Yet, this change is insignificant compared to the comprehensive human impoverishment brought about by thousands of years of suppression of natural living, particularly of natural sexuality. It is only this suppression over thousands of years which has created the mass-psychological soil of fear of authority and submission to it, of incredible humility on the one side and sadistic brutality on the other, and by which the capitalist order of the past 200 years has been able to exist. The fact should not be forgotten, though, that it was socio-economic processes which, thousands of years ago, initiated this change in human structure. It is no longer, then, a problem of machine industry of 200 years standing, but of a human structure of about 5,000 years standing, a structure which thus far has proved incapable of putting the machines to its service. As magnificent and revolutionary as the discovery of the laws of capitalist economy was, it alone is insufficient to solve the problems of human submission to authority.

The core of happiness in life is sexual happiness. Nobody of any political importance has ever dared to point this out. The statement was made, instead, that sexuality was a private matter and had nothing to do with politics. The political reaction thinks otherwise!

Capitalist class morality is against sexuality and thus creates the conflict in the first place. The revolutionary movement eliminates the conflict by first creating a sex-affirmative ideology and then giving it practical forms ... and a new order of sexual living. That is, authoritarian social order and social sexual suppression go hand in hand, and revolutionary "morality" and gratification of the sexual needs go together. "New revolutionary morality" in itself means nothing; it becomes concrete only by the fact of orderly gratification of the needs, not only in the sexual realm. Unless revolutionary ideology recognizes the fact that this is its main concrete content it remains empty talk, in conflict with the real facts.

Black America

Newark

The only limit to the oppression of government is the power with which the people show themselves capable of opposing it.

Conflict may be open or latent; but it always exists since the government does not pay attention to discontent and popular resistance except when it is faced with the danger of insurrection.

When the people meekly submit to the law, or their protests are feeble and confined to words, the government studies its own interests and ignores the needs of the people; when the protests are lively, insistent, threatening, the government depending on whether it is more or less understanding, gives way or resorts to repression. But one always comes back to insurrection, for if the government does not give way, the people will end by rebelling, and if the government does give way, then the people gain confidence in themselves and make ever increasing demands, until such time as the incompatibility between freedom and authority become clear and the violent struggle is engaged.

It is therefore necessary to be prepared, morally and materially, so that when this does happen the people will emerge victorious.

Enrico Malatesta - 1920

And so the words of this Italian anarchist become real again forty years later - in Newark N.J. We must begin to realize that these are no longer riots but rather as Gov. Hughes claimed, acts of "insurrection" - and we must act accordingly. To leave each ghetto at the mercy of the National Guard is becoming more and more tragic. Until the blacks are joined by sections of the white working class they will have to rely on their own strength. Their collective strength - an injury to one should be an injury to all.

While the brothers are being shot in Newark, Black workers are keeping the machine going.

While the brothers are being shot in Newark, Black soldiers are dying to protect "whitey."

While the brothers are being shot in Newark, the other ghettos wait to be attacked next.

Realize this is now a revolution and we need revolutionary solidarity. If they seek to crush our brothers they must crush us all — white and black.

R.A.M.

Finally we must put the pieces together. The same cops who were "unable" to save Malcolm X have now uncovered a "plot" against the life of Roy Wilkins Jr. (NAACP). Those who are themselves murderers now appear as the apprehenders of "murderers," justifying their own crimes while at the same time they seek to crush all opposition. But in attempting to "frame" R.A.M. (Revolutionary Action Movement) they have exposed their own fears. They have created a condition of rebellion and now they seek a way out.

This case represents a new escalation in the war on Black America. Until now they have been content to wait for a so-called "riot" in order to arrest and destroy Black militants but now they have decided to move first, and in this the press has a major role. It must create a climate of hysteria and fear which can give the impression of a crime where in fact none exists. Examine the R.A.M. case closely. They found "weapons" and "subversive" literature which though neither is illegal both have been used as evidence of "guilt." They claim R.A.M. is dedicated to the overthrow of the U.S. Government and therefore those arrested must be guilty. But in fact most of those arrested were not members of R.A.M. and cannot be tied to its policies. But basically we should realize that it is the right of self-defense for the oppressed to seek to overthrow the oppressor. The press has headlined "A Time-Table for Murder" but two days later (in a line buried on page 30) District Attorney Mackel denies there ever was one. The police have charged none with the "murder" plot but the press has implicated (and convicted) the 16. In fact 14 were charged with nothing more than "conspiring to advocate criminal anarchy." A charge so broad as to include all radicals, white and black.

This is not a case of civil rights or of human rights, it is an act of war. Now they are after the blacks, but we are next. Black Americans have appealed to their black brothers to unite or perish: We appeal to all, white and black, here and abroad - We must stand together or we will fall together.

Editors

BLACK MASK

No. 8   OCT. - NOV.   1967   5 Cents

The New Proletariat

The full measure of the black revolt has been only glimpsed in the July days of Newark and Detroit -- a prelude. The revolution looms ahead and the problems are great: theory, organization, tactics, all must be exposed in the glare of the burning ghettoes -- not to explain, but to add fuel, to add a coherence which can bring our objective -- Revolution -- closer.

BLACK MASK

Theory must become a weapon with which we attempt to understand what has happened and affect what will happen. There can be no easy formula no "you do it and we will support you" poses, no substitutes for real thought and action. It is time we examined those frozen concepts of past revolutions -- not to replace them with new "rules" but to find what is worthless and

(cont.)

BLACK MASK

BLACK MASK No. 8 - October/November 1967
The New Proletariat

The full measure of the black revolt has been only glimpsed in the July days of Newark and Detroit — a prelude. The revolution looms ahead and the problems are great: theory, organization, tactics, all must be exposed in the glare of the burning ghettoes — not to explain, but to add fuel, to add a coherence which can bring our objective — Revolution — closer.

Theory must become a weapon with which we attempt to understand what has happened and affect what will happen. There can be no easy formula, no "you do it and we will support you" poses, no substitutes for real thought and action. It is time we examined those frozen concepts of past revolutions - not to replace them with new "rules" but to find what is worthless and what is constant, what has passed and what is possible, while at the same time we must evaluate those ideas being posed today. Revolution is not a popularity contest; it cannot follow our cultural example of a new fad every year, a new star, or a new thrill, it must follow its own dialectic and draw its own conclusion. What is happening today in the search for instant ideology is exactly what Marx exposed as characteristic of capitalist society; reification (thingifying). The only difference is that now the so-called left has also fallen into line. They have objectified revolution: it is no longer a question of social transformation but rather a "thing" to be had by anyone who follows the book, be it Mao's Red Book or Debray's "Revolution Within the Revolution." By anyone who idolizes the proper gods be it Che or "the blacks" — thus satisfying their need for a revolutionary posture while in fact there is no revolution. But isn't it safer that way — the people of the third-world can die for our revolutionary glory, the blacks can carry the weight of our struggle. Witness the New Politics Convention — finally the white liberal has been replaced by his cousin the white radical — could anything be more apparent than their need for capitulation before black demands. What else have they? Obviously many were attempting to make their sincerity concrete but this is at least a new paternalism (the indulgent parent) or at worst a manipulation of black bodies to fight their battles. If the blacks had decided to get together with their brothers first, then the whites had better do the same: they can no longer ride the black panther. Yet revolution has no color barrier: if blacks can do it, whites better learn, for only then will Revolutionary power replace Black Power, revolution replace nationalism.

As revolutionists we must not accept anything without first exposing it to a revolutionary criticism. We must find those values which have motivated us to struggle. If the goal is a social transformation then we cannot accept reform as a basis for our activity, even if it is reform by the gun. And so the fact that people have waged or are waging national liberation struggles is not a replacement for revolutionary perspective. We cannot uncritically support the one without relinquishing our belief in the other. Obviously we support the NLF against American aggression but we must at the same time expect more: it is only the politician, seeking to use others for his purposes, who is unable to criticize for fear of alienating his tool. And so the bullshit left doesn't bat an eye when they read the recently issued platform of the NLF - a platform protecting church property, private property, capital investment, etc., a program designed for the national bourgeoisie, who are leading the struggle but not for the peasants who are waging it. Sure reform is on the agenda but the masses can in the long run gain nothing by reform except the inevitability of another struggle - this time against their own bourgeoisie. Nor is the so-called left capable of criticizing Debray (or Fidel) when they substitute the guerrilla band for the masses. They confuse tactics because they are confused theoretically: they see the part as the whole. Obviously there are advantages to small mobile units (guerrillas) but this is not new. Peoples struggles have taken this form for thousands of years; yet not having made it into an ideology, they were able to adapt it freely to the circumstances and conditions, but always as a part of the mass struggle and not as an end in itself. Strategic mobility is an important part, yet only a part, there must at the same time be mass organizations - not political parties but rather direct organs capable of waging the struggle but also of seizing power; capable of harboring the seeds of a new society within the shell of the old, a role the guerrilla band could not fulfil even if it were successful militarily, for the social transformation necessitates the active and creative role of the masses; they must have power directly in their hands, as did the original Soviets (workers councils) which engineered the overthrow of Tzarist Russia. It is only the proletariat which in seeking its freedom can bring the final blow to the state. For being the backbone of the economy its demand for self-management is dependent upon the complete destruction of all hierarchical systems: their freedom depends on the totality — while at the same time, the totality is dependent on their freedom. Yet we have no intentions of posing 19th or early 20th century conditions as ours. The proletariat was then synonymous with the working class, for at that time the economic basis was industrial — therefore the proletariat: that element which has no power over its own life, while at the same time is the source of power for others — was industrial. But that has changed. Now we have a new proletariat, a proletariat which must not work or demand power in order for the system to function smoothly. It is these cybernetic and automation extras upon whom the system is being built, it is those, to whom life is denied so that others may live, who' will carry the new banner - those to whom burn, baby, burn is the only logical response. No longer will the demands be centered on wages, but rather on power, for the machines can do the work, but the question is - Who benefits? As the demand of the industrial proletariat was for workers' control, so the demand of the new proletariat will be for non-workers' control. All power to the workers' and non-workers' councils, for their goals are not contrary but rather the same: and their realization the final victory of man.

Culture and Revolution

Bourgeois culture is the enemy as is the bourgeois system itself. Not only the Rembrandts and Goethes but the modernists also will find themselves on the scrapheap of western culture. Our history merely teaches us how to succeed at the expense of others. No artist can be anything other than the bedmate of the business man and the imperialist. Therefore it is not enough to institute a revolution of style and content (which only perpetuates the culture by giving it new blood): the culture itself must be destroyed. For no matter how dissident the revolt, the bourgeoisie enjoys it; it creates subjects for his magazine culture - he absorbs the scene without living it. And so his lust for distraction is satisfied by every multiplying shit-isms - pop-op-mini-nart-funk-etc. A whole new business has grown on the end of culture announced by Dada and surrealism; a new slick non-culture, Institutionalized Dada. Free verse - already declared obsolete in 1910 by Futurists; happenings - theatricized Dada acts; "underground" publications (Oracle, E.V.O., Int. Times) an art nouveau religious revival replete with saints, gods and gurus (Leary, Ginsberg etc.) and the latest gimmick - the canned pornography of the Fugs and psychedelic profiteering.

Though the early movements (futurism, Dada, Surrealism etc.) were vital as a spirit, a state of fury, their degeneracy into òbject art was already inherent in their safe adoption of the "ism." All "isms" and ideologies are the rendering of thought which is alive into formulae which are easy substitutes for real activity. We need to finally clear the air: the "ism" is itself the enemy.

"Without any reservations the revolution must be entirely aggressive can only be entirely aggressive," A. Breton/Counter Attack. And so our aggression turns on you Andre Breton. You allowed yourself to be canonized; you the great declaimer of the "high image." But even worse are the defilers of surrealism: Sartre and Camus, Litterateurs in the "true" tradition. Existentialism: a disguise for non-existence. No, Sartre, you will not be saved by sitting on the tribunals in judgement of the west while you yourself as philosopher/novelist are the west. But Camus you disgust us: your death has cheated us of the pleasure of killing you ourselves.

But it is not enough to talk: we need to place dynamite at the very foundations themselves, not just tear off its branches. Art as alienation; the inevitable outcome of a culture (itself the result of a socio-economic system) which is divorced from real life. Nothing short of a complete social revolution can end the separation which exists between culture and life; the two are inseparable. Can we accept a regime as revolutionary which pays "artists" twice as much as workers and this in the midst of a "cultural revolution" (Mao's China), or a regime which celebrates its revolution (?) with a Tchaikovsky recital attended in full tails by the ruling class (Cuba) — or even more basic can we accept any system as revolutionary which perpetuates one-man management as opposed to collective rule? Can any system which is economically based on hierarchical organization be free from the cultural hierarchy of artists and the tyranny of experts?

Yet we ourselves must not fall into the trap. Either we are propelled to action or it is meaningless.

Yvonne De Nigris	Anne Ryder	Jenny Dicken	Everett Shapiro
Ron Hahne	Carol Verlaan	Benn Morea	Tony Verlaan
Janice Morea	David Wise	John Myers	Stuart Wise

The absurdity of our civilization has become spectacular; even the attempts to alter it only reproduce that which should be destroyed (destruction being the one form which carries its own conclusion).

To repeat ourselves when we can clearly see the past is nonsense. We must realize the utter futility of both the political revolution which only seeks new masters (and therefore new revolutions) and the cultural revolution which changes only the product and not the means of production. Dada was not Dada. And the Diggers are less than Dada. Their theater of the streets can be found in Zurich and Paris 1916-21; having failed then it is already doomed. The mistake remains constant. The entirety of life must be changed and theatrics are not enough. Sure "everything is free." But how do we make concrete what is only ideology? The question is one of power - Power over our lives - and that means now.

So back to Zurich 1916; Lenin and Tzara chessmates, evening comes and they separate, one to formulate Bolshevism the other Dada — yet they were both to be failures in their success: one becoming the politician/dictator the other poet/artist, partial in view they could not be total in result. Bad then — it is worse now when our dreams and the possibilities of technology are so close. We must not accept the repetition being planned by the left (heirs to Bolshevism) or the Diggers (as neo-Dada); we must see the absolute necessity for a synthesis, one which will leave our culture and civilization in a state beyond repair. One which in its totality is the construction/destruction, thought/action posed before only in fragments.

B. M.

Children Protruding from the Earth

"Fragments of clothing, books and furniture flew so high that all in the vicinity knew the school was bombed. Students were blasted. Many were buried in the earth. I was among those buried alive. I was dug out later and was brought to consciousness. There was nothing left but a bomb crater, 55 feet wide and 21 feet deep. Everything was levelled. Parts of the children were protruding from the earth. We found their heads 20 yards away. Their bowels and intestines were scattered everywhere. Two of my children were spattered on a palm tree and hung from it. Children were pressed to the trench walls. Blood filled their trenches. Children clutched their books tightly to their chests. The books were smeared in blood and ink. Some of them could speak a little when dug out. Then blood shot from their mouths, due to their crushed organs and they died. One little girl, Hoang Thai Nha, twelve, could only be recognized and identified by her rubber shoes. Six of the children were too mutilated to be recognisable to the parents. One dug out became conscious and asked how many of her friends died before hemorrhaging.

Little Hung's body was found on top of unfinished poems he had written, along with a notebook of paintings.He aspired to be a poet, painter and composer. His poems, paintings and songs are all signed: 'Composer, Dinh Hung'. He was thirteen."

Reprinted from:

Bertrand Russell Peace Foundation Bulletin

342 West 84 Street, New York, New York 10024

... you see d.r. they are murdering the children we didnt have time to become.. i cant read your poems anymore d.r. i cant read any poems anymore. perhaps its because i know you had to return to write them, you once asked ' how much do we have to give them, before they understand' these are beautiful poems d.r. but this is not our home, it is time to move, white horses painted black at night into their minds/ no holiness, no mysticism, it is a game of the universe and i am tired of the illusions. my brothers and sisters are weeping and frightened in the darkness of their skulls. I am tired of travelling only to find names in the dust. It is time to move again lets say inward toward the city of the sun. The falcons at our side. So many wonderful words/ in travelling have you noticed any frightened spirits of vietnamese children wandering in the darkness ... you see its like they created a fear machine & forgot how to turn it off & now they keep trying to convince everyone that fear is the only way and ah, oh those insipid naive love-ins flower children wilting in jails, flower children wilting under the lights of the inner suns ...

oh d.r. you see its all kinds of things like when i was reading a recent issue of M. of O. & it sed Comandante Hernando Gonzalez age 23 killed in action colombian fighting for the freedom of his country dead age 23 dead age 23 dead age 23 and in america children are being murdered SLOWLY fighting for the write to scribble a few lines of poetry ... on the sun ... can you understand? no matter how you play the game It Is War and in America we need more than words white horses painted black for me perhaps egyptians need different mirages small boats on the four rivers/ make certain you are well armed/eyed/ & the guardian of the arits

ask them for directions /
sumtimes they dont know the answers
& pass you on to a higher authority
Introduction? Hernandes Gonzalez age 23 is dead age 23 is dead age 23
d.a.levy/cleveland ohio

Oct 21: A Peace or Totality

The present system of death and oppression cannot exist without waging war. U.S. napalm is already falling in Latin America, and to be sure, the U.S. government would not fall short of napalming its own black population. To bring "peace" to Vietnam will only bring war elsewhere.

The impotence of the peace movement has served America well - by channeling possible revolutionary elements into a safe form of protestation; by assuaging the guilt of the monster itself. But the peace movement is dead! And we must make sure it is replaced by a living revolutionary movement which will end forever atrocities such as Vietnam.

300,000 strong "peace marching" within police barricades on 5th Avenue (April 15th) will accomplish nothing. But the 10,000 who broke from the "legal" parade route and marched through the streets of Manhattan to show their determination and defy the police - the Japanese students of the Zengakuren whose forceful demonstrations have totally blocked the streets of Tokyo - the oppressed peoples of the ghettoes who have risen against the system - these hold a revolutionary consciousness no matter how embryonic.

We must develop a tradition of militant demonstration. Perhaps only then will some of the futility of today's movement disappear. There can exist no peace under this system. But worse, there can be no real life! The poverty of life is apparent - the walls are crumbling!

Let us become Revolutionists. Let us insist that all power be in the hands of the people, whether they be American or Vietnamese.

J. M.

BLACK MASK

No. 9   JAN.- FEB. 1968   5 Cents

"These smut sheets, are today's Molotov cocktails thrown at respectability and decency in our nation. . . . They encourage depravity and irresponsibility, and they nurture a breakdown in the continued capacity of the government to conduct an orderly and constitutional society."
Rep. Joe Pool (House Un-American Activities Comm.)

BLACK MASK No.9 · January/February 1968

*"These smut sheets, are today's Molotov cocktails thrown at
respectability and decency in our nation. ... They encourage
depravity and irresponsibility, and they nurture a breakdown in the
continued capacity of the government to conduct an orderly and
constitutional society."*

Rep. Joe Pool (House Un-American Activities Comm.)

The State of the Union and the Dissolution of the State

"Our constitutional system is becoming a shambles and anarchy " (Sen.
Kuchal). "Advocating a shift from dissent to resistance, a small but vociferous
body of young and immature older war objectors has begun to incite acts of
anarchy that could destroy precisely the values they profess to defend" (N.Y.
Times Editorial). "The right of dissent is integral to a free society; otherwise it
lapses into tyranny. But there must be limits to dissent when it takes the form of
action; otherwise the result is anarchy" (Sydney Hook, N.Y. Times Magazine).

"Those who protest and those who become discouraged have to realize we've been through difficult problems before and we'll surmount them. The answer to the problems is in our society not in anarchy to overthrow our system" (Sen. Robert Kennedy). "Those who use the presence of President Johnson or of the Secretary of State everytime they appear as an excuse for riotous or violent behavior are endangering the legitimate expression of dissent by inviting anarchy, that among other things is self-defeating" (N.Y. Times).

For the past few months the spector of anarchy has haunted our fine establishment. They long for the good old days of impotent dissent. But those days are gone. The summer of black revolt has become the winter of white resistance: and hopefully what may yet be reached is a point where black revolt and white resistance become one - fused in the heat of revolution.

Yet the struggle will be long - and already the Government is seeking to suppress this new movement with the threat of immediate military draft for the "law-breakers." But that will prove to be a double edged sword, for the revolt of the troops has also begun. Besides the individual acts of refusal to serve in Vietnam and a growing number of desertions, the reality of MUTINY has hit Ft. Hood, Texas; this follows the report last year of a riot at Ft. Dix, N.J. and the report of a troop insurrection in the northern sector of South Vietnam. The troops have begun to serve notice that they will no longer be willing cannon-fodder.

Poor whites have also shown a real potential for radical activity. Nothing more clearly shows where their interests lie than their joining with blacks in the Detroit riots and the arrest of several white snipers. The peoples want power. And we are the people.

And now, the white (student) resistance; the immediate threat to the peace of our beloved dictator. We can, and we must, expect the full weight of the establishment to be brought to bear against this potential rebellion: from Joe Pool and the hawks to Bobby Kennedy and the liberals; from the "peace" leadership to the "revolutionaries" who counsel restraint. But the peoples want power, and we are the people.

Editors

BUT THIS IS ABSURD

WE DON'T WANT TO BECOME NIGGERS

we don't want no nigger demonstrations: lot of black mothers running through the streets. No dignity. No higher aspirations. Burning. Stealing stuff. Throwing things. Getting beaten. Whole lot of black shit.

WHITE IS NICE

Nice white demonstrations is nice: thinking about things, making decisions, organizing marshals, planning mobile tactics, confrontations with the police,

"Those who protest and those who become discouraged have to realize we've been through difficult problems before and we'll surmount them. The answer to the problems is in our society not in anarchy to overthrow our system" (Sen. Robert Kennedy). "Those who use the presence of President Johnson or of the Secretary of State everytime they appear as an excuse for riotous or violent behavior are endangering the legitimate expression of dissent by inviting anarchy, that among other things is self-defeating" (N.Y. Times).

For the past few months the spector of anarchy has haunted our fine establishment. They long for the good old days of impotent dissent. But those days are gone. The summer of black revolt has become the winter of white resistance: and hopefully what may yet be reached is a point where black revolt and white resistance become one - fused in the heat of revolution.

Yet the struggle will be long - and already the Government is seeking to suppress this new movement with the threat of immediate military draft for the "law-breakers." But that will prove to be a double edged sword, for the revolt of the troops has also begun. Besides the individual acts of refusal to serve in Vietnam and a growing number of desertions, the reality of MUTINY has hit Ft. Hood, Texas; this follows the report last year of a riot at Ft. Dix, N.J. and the report of a troop insurrection in the northern sector of South Vietnam. The troops have begun to serve notice that they will no longer be willing cannon-fodder.

Poor whites have also shown a real potential for radical activity. Nothing more clearly shows where their interests lie than their joining with blacks in the Detroit riots and the arrest of several white snipers. The peoples want power. And we are the people.

And now, the white (student) resistance; the immediate threat to the peace of our beloved dictator. We can, and we must, expect the full weight of the establishment to be brought to bear against this potential rebellion: from Joe Pool and the hawks to Bobby Kennedy and the liberals; from the "peace" leadership to the "revolutionaries" who counsel restraint. But the peoples want power, and we are the people.

Editors

BUT THIS IS ABSURD

WE DON'T WANT TO BECOME NIGGERS

we don't want no nigger demonstrations: lot of black mothers running through the streets. No dignity. No higher aspirations. Burning. Stealing stuff. Throwing things. Getting beaten. Whole lot of black shit.

WHITE IS NICE

Nice white demonstrations is nice: thinking about things, making decisions, organizing marshals, planning mobile tactics, confrontations with the police, risking one's life (sort of) for higher things (aware of precedents), building a movement; stop the war, end of the draft, etc. This is much nicer; more intellectual; whiter.

LET US AVOID ALL THE LEADS TO NIGGERHOOD.

Stay on the right side of the TV set: watch them little black mothers running their ass off, undignified, but athletic, knocking things over, getting clubbed stupid. They have a nigger fate in store for them. Getting beat is good for niggers. It confirms their niggerhood. It fits in with ghettoes, junk, filthy ugly tenements. Niggers get beat all the time. Look at that one, running, caught, sullen, not saying anything... we could never be sullen like that. We know what his fate is. He will become more and more nigger until he either kills himself, or is killed: both fates amounting essentially to the same.

WE WANT TO PLAY GAMES

Games are liberating.

Games are Utopian.

We become embodied in doing. But doing is a trap. One is forced to choose between a doing which is not a doing, a doing which does not have the feel of doing, a doing which does on their level of unreality; and, on the other hand a doing which is a breaking away from that level, a doing which is liberating... and for which you get your head busted. No other alternatives: trapped in a nigger trap inspite of ourselves.

T. N.

Demonstrations:
A Theory of Practice and the Practice of Theory

Demonstrations exist as a means of struggle; the question is one of developing revolutionary consciousness and not one of moral outrage. We are not outraged by what this system does - we expect the worst. We are, instead, enraged and seek its destruction. Yet we are at an uneasy juncture: for the bourgeoisification of the struggle must be reversed but we have yet to develop a mass base as substitute. The Japanese Zengakauren has no need for bourgeois liberal "sympathy," they have the support of the workers. If we are ever to develop a form which has meaning and content for the masses of working and poor then we must think and act as revolutionists (and not as outraged moralists). We must speak to the suppression of their lives as related to the oppression of others (e.g. the poorer whites will put up less opposition to black "riots" than to the "peace" movement - they understand the first as a revolt against a suppressed life whereas the latter is an exercise in bourgeois morality). But the reverse is not, as some would suppose, to concentrate on an anti-imperialist struggle; not because we are not anti-imperialist, but for the masses within the belly of imperialism this can only serve again as bourgeois morality. The essence of revolutionary struggle has always been the demand for power to quantitatively and qualitatively change our lives: therefore it is not a question of sympathy with the downtrodden, as only the bourgeoisie can have, but a question of identification: we are the downtrodden. And the most advanced form of "demonstration" will be the one which unifies theory and practice: revolution.

If we are ever to reach this point of coherence then we have got to deal with the present situation in a way which contributes to that end. Not by refusing to join the struggle because it hasn't reached our level but rather by moving the struggle to that level.

The bankruptcy of the present "peace" leadership is everywhere apparent, and they seek nothing more than to demonstrate this bankruptcy. At meetings called to plan the "stop the draft week" they constantly expressed the fear that the demonstration might lose the focus of the induction center and therefore the issue of the draft. Being confused theoretically they could not hope to be correct tactically - there is no issue, if it is not everything. The government understands this better than we do. On Oct. 21st, while the Pentagon was being guarded by 8,000 troops, 20,000 troops guarded the city of Washington itself. The government feared what only a few of us had yet to understand - the city, and the colonization of life, would be the logical target. This may also be seen in the campus struggle. Here the emphasis is on an anti-Dow-CIA-imperialism. But as the president of I.B.M. recently asked "why all the fuss over Dow, every business in America is profiting over the war." Conversely every "Job" in America is "imperialist:" and in the full sense of the word - our lives are colonized. The only value this diversion has for students is to protect the illusion that there are still other possibilities in America for a real existence. There are none: and to realize this, is to realize revolution.

B. M.

We seek a form of total revolt which transcends both art and politics

Revolution and Psychoanalysis and Revolution

There exists a deeply rooted structural formation in the relationship between individual and social character structure. Nevertheless, revolutionists have failed to recognize the significance of this for the revolutionary movement itself, or if they have recognized it they either minimize its meaning or they transform it into a new revolutionary principle of leadership.

But our problem is precisely the understanding of the relationship of those submissive aspects of character structure in periods of social collapse to both the remnants of the old society and the growing struggle against it. Suffice it to say that the impossibility of living under the old social order does not guarantee in itself the destruction of the old character structure, nor even the political success of the revolutionary movement. The carrying over of deeply rooted bourgeois character attitudes into the revolutionary movement signifies the weakening of that movement. But then, this means that the revolutionary movement faces more than political problems, or that the political problems are much deeper than they have so far been understood to be in Marxist theory. The bourgeois order is rooted in character structure, and character structure is the link between the bourgeois order and the revolutionary movement. It makes a sad paraphrase of Marx's dictum: the revolutionary movement contains within itself the seeds of its own destruction; the old order is contained within the womb of the new.

At this point we necessarily enter upon the domain of psychoanalysis. As might be expected, our enemies are none other than the psychoanalysists themselves. It is not by chance that psychoanalysis has gone through as many ideological splits, polemical intrigues and organizational manoeuvres as "Marxism." The same characterological submissiveness that inhibits revolutionists from carrying to completion their attack on the bourgeois social order inhibits analysists from systematically attacking the bourgeois character structure.

Furthermore, there is an internal, essential relationship between character structure and social structure. Upon the synthesis of these two modes of life depends the the fate of the revolutionary movement.

Wilhelm Reich took up the revolutionary challenge implicit in the clinical findings of psychoanalysis. For the first time psychoanalysis left the parlors of the bourgeoisie and entered the streets of the proletariat. It was no longer a theory resting on a foundation of illusory individualism, but linked itself up with the great social struggles of the time. To Reich the revolutionist, psychoanalysis was meaningless unless it helped to comprehend the struggle against capitalism; to Reich the scientist, psychoanalysis was a myth if it could not help explain the contradictions of social life.

Reich's psychoanalytic sword cut both ways: Marxism was criticized for its failure to understand either mass neurotic suffering or its political implications. Marxism had claimed to struggle on behalf of the oppressed, yet the oppression of daily life - the sexual misery of the masses - was a problem not only untouched but also unmentioned in either Marxist theory or Marxist practice. At the same time Marxism had scarcely understood the basis for mass submission to poverty and oppression, and had been thereby condemned to stumble half blind through the swamp of capitalist oppression. Since the key to submissiveness lay in the understanding of the role of sexual repression in its formation, Marxism lacked a revolutionary weapon which was immediately both theoretical and practical.

On the other hand, psychoanalysis was criticized for its failure to take seriously the problem of the prevention of the neurosis. Analysts were taking their bourgeois patients by ones and twos while neurotics by the tens of million were being produced by parents, educators and politicians. The disastrous social conditions of capitalist society conceived of in its totality, is the source of the neuroses; a therapy which ignores this is not only of almost no human significance; more important, such an individual perspective inevitably becomes an ideological prop for the existing order.

We have now come to the crux of the matter; the development of a dialectical understanding of character and social structure. This must explain the disastrous failure of Marxism and socialism as well as develop a revolutionary understanding of being human. The latter must not become merely a problem to be solved after the revolution, as Reich used to put it in his earlier work. Rather, the revolutionary conception of sexuality must become the active principle of the revolutionary movement. The latter must struggle to break down the repressive structures in itself that keep it not only from living, but from the revolutionary struggle itself. In the last analysis, only that revolutionary movement that finds the way to express the actual needs of life in its daily existence - that is, one which reverses the dynamic of repression in itself - can accomplish the necessary destruction of class society, repression and civilization.

The content of class society can be expressed in the uncomfortable fact that human life is perverted in every sphere of its activity; thinking as well as doing, hating as well as loving, seeing as well as feeling. Marx, in his early writings, focused on this perversion. Alienation was not for him the deliberate euphemism that it has become for today's radical intellectuals. Moreover, insofar as psychoanalysis has revealed to us the hitherto unfathomed depth and almost limitless extensions of the repression of life in capitalist society, we may in good conscience dispense with the term altogether. Instead, we will at all times struggle to grasp alienation in the fullness of its dead concreteness.

The perversions of living are not whimsical: they are integral parts of society as a whole. The fact that certain pathologies (which are truly perversions of life) appear to exist in an entirely individual way having no relationship to the social and political structure of society is a consequence of the intensity of repression as well as deeply rooted fears of comprehending the profound misery of our lives.

Socialist and liberal conceptions of being human are almost indistinguishable. It follows therefore that contemporary socialism is little more than an abstract schema of social revolution attached to a very bourgeois conception of the needs of human beings. It is our task now to get behind the apparent needs of man in capitalist society to the core of ourselves. Only on this basis is it possible to struggle for our own liberation.

Moreover, the driving force of revolution is not economic misery, automatically blossoming forth in political struggle; but rather the contradiction between the possibility of being human and the reality of oppression - of human, not economic misery. We may add that economic misery is bound up with human suffering, but it is only insofar as the worker feels himself as human that he struggles against his inhuman condition.

This trend in Marx's thought has been obliterated by the efflorescence of egoism and fetishism in the socialist movement. In this early work are to be found the elements of a revolutionary analytical psychology. The failure to develop such a psychology necessarily left Marxism hanging in the air. Marx described alienation in human terms; but he could only develop the economic side of it. The structure of character — and therewith the inner structure of society itself — remained unexplored. Thus, unable to explain the dynamic relationship of human beings to the products of their estranged labor, Marxism degenerated into economic fatalism: without saying so explicitly, Marxists saw economic collapse as the cause of revolution, but they never understood that the collapse of a system, and its failure to satisfy the needs of fetishistic consumption, does not of itself lead to the consciousness of the need to destroy fetishism.

Marx spoke of alienation, but the determinate content of alienation is suppression. Taken in this way it has already a dynamic significance. The revolutionary potential of a theory of repression is that, driven to its limit, it must yield up its secret: the fullness of being.

But our effort is undermined by the very means we must use to continue it: language. And language is not the only tyrant lurking in disguise. The horror of all our past hopes is contained in the fact that socialism, both as movement and ideology, has been as puritanical and life-denying as the language and structures of science itself. Socialists, so crushed in the misery of their own lives, brought their self-denial into the conceptions and methods of the liberation movement itself. The tragedy of it all, is that while the form was liberation, the content was repression.

Thus, we must find our way back to the body; language must be made to destroy itself; we must find a way of communicating our feeling of our bodies, subverting all the scientific and historical categories that have so far only been agents of repression. More precisely, we must be aware of the significance of scientific description. It is valid only insofar as we are enslaved; it is because we are not. If we comprehend this then we are already in a position to resurrect our bodies from the clutches of bourgeois order. Nevertheless, the conditions for this resurrection is the development of a sex-revolutionary movement against the routine and order of bourgeois "life." The condition of liberation - in the present - is the social affirmation of life. This is so because of the nature of repression itself. All attempts at individual liberation therefore actually fail because the problem is one of the socio-character structure, not of some mysterious inner neurotic tendency which exists in a merely external relation to all that is "outside" of one's self.

The great value of Freud's and Reich's work is that it proceeds from the premise that something has been repressed, forgotten, almost lost. It is not a question of statistics: what percentage of women are frigid? or how may people are socially handicapped by neuroses? or how many suffer lack of ego gratification? These are conceptions of a superficial bourgeois psychology. Freud and Reich went much deeper. Not a single human being who is raised in a patriarchal authoritarian culture is in touch with the fullness of his body's sexuality.

In this we have a critique of the bourgeois order itself. The mass misery, the periodic breakthroughs of mass hysteria - the willingness of people to become cannon-fodder in imperialist wars - these conditions are neither accidental nor superficial, but are inevitable in a culture of repression.

For Freud, sadism, masochism, greed, miserliness, submissiveness, aggressive morality, etc. are results of repression of infantile sexuality. The sum total of these characteristics accurately describe bourgeois society. Civilization, according to Freud, was based on such repression. Therefore the revolutionary project is clear: the liberation of life is bound up with the destruction of civilization.

JPM

Fragments of Revolutionary Totality
(1)

The "poverty" against which man has been constantly struggling, is not merely the poverty of material goods; in fact, in industrially advanced countries the disappearance of material poverty has revealed the poverty of existence itself. In cybernetic society it is the mediocrity of existence; the deprivation of a real intellectual, emotional, sexual or social life: the impoverishment of every dimension and every moment of man's existence; that finally defines the contemporary meaning of the "poverty" of our lives.

The struggle against this condition must be total, because the poverty against which we are struggling is total: it is the repressive organization of life in its entirety; depriving us of the opportunity to be fully human. And when it is life in it entirety (literally the planet and species) that is degraded by an encompassing culture predicated on Death, then the only struggles which we can afford to call "revolutionary" are those which seek revolution in Totality: the creation of a new life in a new environment which we ourselves must construct.

We have been forced to see that wherever the revolution of ideology appears to "succeed" it reveals that it is not revolutionary at all: it does not change the context or content of life. Every historical change, at best, has been radical reform: Jacobinism, Bolshevism, Maoism or Castroismo: all have reorganized men's lives in one or a few of their aspects, but they fear the transformation of life in its entirety which begins when men dare to rule their own lives — the an-archos (Greek), meaning without rulers.

(2)

All of past revolutionary thought has been confined to the problems of dividing the surplus of labor and distributing the scarcity of goods and services. For them the best form of society seemed to be the kind of socialism which came up with the most rational answers to these questions. And because of this the ultimate goal of their practice, of tactics and strategy, was the problem of seizing power, grasping control of the decision making process (politics) in order to re-organize society according to ideology.

But the very basis of revolution has changed, and only the general consciousness lags behind: we have not dared to dream high enough, seeking only to grasp that which is immediately beyond our reach, and thus succumbing even in our most sublime moments, to the limitations which have been imposed upon us from outside by those who manipulate our lives; those who once dared to call themselves our "Masters."

Our problem is not the seizure of power and the establishment of socialism: for we have been forced to see that what is revolutionary about change is that people begin to take control of their own lives in the struggle to throw off that which suppresses them. For the present the ultimate tactical question must be, not the seizure of power, but its dissolution! REVOLUTION BEGINS WHEN PEOPLE TAKE CONTROL OF THEIR OWN LIVES.

the TOTALIST

PO Box 698 Stuyvesant Sta. NYC 10009.

BLACK MASK

No. 10   APRIL MAY   5 Cents

Berlin Dada

"EVERYONE CAN BE A DADAIST"

In Berlin 1918 Huelsenbeck broke with Zurich and Paris Dada. As a dynamic revolt, Dada could not be categorically bound, least of all to the category of abstract art into which Tzara had led it.

Zurich and Paris introduced the tradition of fashionable nihilistic non-art. Berlin Dada, placed on a revolutionary basis, transcended non-art in a totally undifferentiated attack. Every form of revolutionary subversion was encouraged: hysteria, madness, abuse, black humor etc. It was a series of immediately comprehensible activities within the reach of everyone, ranging from spontaneous nonsensical gestures to photomontages, which like the crossed eyed portrait of Beethoven are in the most obvious bad taste. Berlin Dada at its best recognized the self-defeating function of an art which appealed to freedom locked in a formal prison: for art purifies, through catharsis, what should be seized directly-- life. An alienated seriousness can only respond to the esthetics of detached observation. Intuitively, Berlin Dada was alive to the death ot all art as expression sublimated into painting, music, theater, writing, poetry, film etc. All sacrosanct activities were magnificently negated and real life recognized and affirmed.

Like early Surrealism, although on a more direct, day to day level, Berlin Dada caught the scent of apocalypse-- the end of all those thousands of years of unculture-- repressed with genius-- the end of history-- the assassination of fixed time-- the end of anxiety-- the third great turning point in the world:

first: an event in geological history

second: the beginning of civilization

third: the highest point of civilization(return from alienation)

Heraclitus: "Homer should be turned out of the ranks & flogged"

Huelsenbeck: "What is German culture? (Answer: SHIT)"

Pythagoras: "beans are the cause of all revolutions"

Huelsenbeck: "Riots in the vegetable market"

Surrealists and Shamans become inseperable.

THE ABSOLUTE REFUSAL & THE GREAT WORLD REVOLUTION

Beyond this is the dawn of a paradise of delight: where our passions spring live in a disruption of our homes, food, tempests, motorways; the point at which Marinetti's "the earth our sky, the stars our pavements", and Rimbaud's "feed hungers on meadows of sound" meet. (continued inside)

Lasime Tushinde Mbilashaka

H. RAP BROWN FROM PRISON

Parish Prison

New Orleans, La.

2/21/68

Being a man is the continuing battle of one's life and one loses a bit of manhood with every stale compromise to the authority of any power in which one does not believe.

No slave should die a natural death. There is a point where caution ends and cowardice begins.

For everyday I am imprisoned I will refuse both food and water. My hunger is for the Liberation of my people. My thirst is for the ending of oppression.

I am a political prisoner, jailed for my belief that Black People must be free. The Government has taken a position true to its fascist nature: Those who we cannot convert, we must silence. This government has become the enemy of Mankind.

Death can no longer alter our path to Freedom. For our people, Death has been the only known exit from slavery and oppression. We must open others.   (continued inside)

BLACK

BLACK MASK No. 10 - April/May 1968

Berlin Dada
"EVERYONE CAN BE A DADAIST"

In Berlin 1918 Huelsenbeck broke with Zurich and Paris Dada. As a dynamic revolt, Dada could not be categorically bound, least of all to the category of abstract art into which Tzara had led it.

Zurich and Paris introduced the tradition of fashionable nihilistic non-art. Berlin Dada, placed on a revolutionary basis, transcended non-art in a totally undifferentiated attack. Every form of revolutionary subversion was encouraged: hysteria, madness, abuse, black humor etc. It was a series of immediately comprehensible activities within the reach of everyone, ranging from spontaneous nonsensical gestures to photomontages, which like the crossed eyed portrait of Beethoven are in the most obvious bad taste. Berlin Dada at its best recognized the self-defeating function of an art which appealed to freedom locked in a formal prison: for art purifies, through catharsis, what should be seized directly - life. An alienated seriousness can only respond to the esthetics of detached observation. Intuitively, Berlin Dada was alive to the death of all art as expression sublimated into painting, music, theater, writing, poetry, film etc. All sacrosanct activities were magnificently negated and real life recognized and affirmed.

Like early Surrealism, although on a more direct, day to day level, Berlin Dada caught the scent of apocalypse - the end of all those thousands of years of unculture - repressed with genius - the end of history - the assassination of fixed time - the end of anxiety - the third great turning point in the world:

first: an event in geological history
second: the beginning of civilization
third: the highest point of civilization (return from alienation)
Heraclitus: "Homer should be turned out of the ranks and flogged"
Huelsenbeck "What is German culture? (Answer: SHIT)"
Pythagoras: "Beans are the cause of all revolutions"
Huelsenbeck: "Riots in the vegetable market"
Surrealists and Shamans become inseparable.

THE ABSOLUTE REFUSAL & THE GREAT WORLD REVOLUTION

Beyond this is the dawn of a paradise of delight: where our passions spring live in a disruption of our homes, food, tempests, motorways; the point at which Marinetti's "the earth our sky, the stars our pavements," and Rimbaud's "feed hungers on meadows of sound" meet.

Berlin Dada sought deliverance from an intolerable world in the healing frenzy of direct possession. Not art but all the organs of individuality: hearing, tasting, feeling, touching, smelling - a super sensuality - the prolonged kiss and the handshake, dreaming, day-dreaming, play, perversion, disease, stealing (just take things, they're free), madness, hysteria, and violence - "The only adequate form of expression."

It is the barbaric disintegration which is the precursor of the poetry of tomorrow.

"I refuse to examine the pros and cons of my arguments."

Johann Baader: schizophrenic, becomes the key figure of Berlin Dada. He is Tzara's "Idiot" transcended: the Idiot/Madman/Guerrilla in life - the man without aim or prospects, the "lowest" of all, the shit of America. Tzara, the man of letters was horrified because Baader is for real. Confronted with the non-intelligence of Baader, Tzara who said "intelligence is found on the streets" was appalled.

Hugnet wrote: "Baader's was a special case of coming to the revolution through individualism and madness."

Baader rides a white horse into **Parliament.** Baader derealizes death (death the most potent form of social coercion) in a magnificent flight from taste and personal responsibility: Inviting 3,000 people to his wife's funeral (who he loved dearly), smiling he shaves off half his beard while her body is lowered into the grave. This act is equaled only by Franz Jung's hi-jacking of a German battleship as a present for the embarrassed Russian Bolsheviks.

This is Berlin Dada. Like everything else it was forced to die when the revolutionary prospects died and its energy was diverted into the forced acceptance of old forms. But at one point their cultural rejection extended to all ideology (bourgeois and orthodox Marxist). Some like the brothers Heartfield and Herzefelde were DISCIPLINED to work with Spartacus (the most libertarian of past proletarian movements). But the rest, rejected by 'professional,' 'political' revolutionaries as 'voluptuaries' were too radical for their time.

PATENT MEDICINES FOR EVERYTHING. LENIN? A LITTLE CHEMIST (W. Mehring)

Huelsenbeck's programme - a fantastic flip into the present called for "progressive unemployment" in a situation where machines would do all the work, and where man, for the first time, would be free to "fulfil himself." In an automated environment, the environment of the technological utopianists, what need for a repressive reality?

THE FUTURE IS MACHINES AND MADNESS

But the Dadaists were unable to appreciate the terror a work based society would feel at the approach of an age of leisure, play and abundance. For when society is faced with the dissolution of its principal pre-occupation, work, it shows all the symptoms of a massive, collective nervous breakdown. The "security" that society offered in work is rapidly disappearing. Automation threatens all class divisions. Thus the question; what is man to do with his leisure, ends in a revolutionary critique of culture. Marx never broached the question of culture, for in the 19th century, culture still could maintain a separation from everyday existence. Art had yet to be transcended through Dada and Surrealism into life. And the traditional left, quite disastrously ignorant of this factor, limits life and revolution everywhere.

Free time would mean the rehabilitation of the flesh: the transfigured body delighting in the full life of the body. But organized free time, passive leisure; leisure as relaxation, the interim state between work and sleep, remains antagonistic to positive fulfilment. It is the Hollywoodization of the end of high culture. The passive consumer leisure demanded from media like T.V., film, gadgetry etc. It is the institutionalization of emptiness - from multi media, music and painting, dancing and film, film and theater, weightless inflatable chairs and coloured ripple sculpture. But the novelty wears off and "new" and more "daring" effects are sought after the raison d'etre of 'free" T.V., 'free" cinema, laser beam 3D. Draw lines in your mind or 'artistically' programme computers. February's "Art In America" suggested we play games (controlled games of course, isolated onanistic games and obscure equations). Neurotic regression to childhood hobbies: a life spent playing with an electric train.

If not that, "freely" move through your own alienation: from poet to film-maker, to father, to architect, to big business. Total pseudo-man.

At this point in history, the "popular" success of Berlin Dada is assured. It is touted from anti-universities through the underground press, to the lush art mags and the Havana cultural conference. All the world will soon be able to accept the distorted image of Berlin Dada. Synthetic play in exchange for the transformation of a sterile existence into lived creativity. A closed world of game objects (e.g. baseball and the model electric train) as a substitute for the free play as life itself.

But it could be in no other way. Late industrial society must constantly seek to control and absorb radical aggression. In an ever ready state of total mobilization against all possibilities, it poisons life from the cradle to the grave.

But Berlin Dada released a libidinal energy capable of revolutionizing reality. With the conditions for freedom (a non-work based society) within our grasp, the play instinct is the ascendant principle and the vehicle of liberation. Thus, what Huelsenbeck wrote in 1918 requires further elaboration:

"In Germany, Dadaism became political, it drew the ultimate consequences of its position and renounced art completely."

And now we must pass through the end of art into politics, equipped with the play instinct in order to destroy politics. It is the sensuousness of the true play instinct which presupposes a Total Revolution in life, perception and feeling.

David & Stuart Wise/London.

Lasime Tushinde Mbilashaka

H. RAP BROWN FROM PRISON

Parish Prison
New Orleans, La.
2/21/68

Being a man is the continuing battle of one's life and one loses a bit of manhood with every stale compromise to the authority of any power in which one does not believe.

No slave should die a natural death. There is a point where caution ends and cowardice begins.

For everyday I am imprisoned I will refuse both food and water. My hunger is for the Liberation of my people. My thirst is for the ending of oppression.

I am a political prisoner, jailed for my belief that Black People must be free. The Government has taken a position true to its fascist nature: Those who we cannot convert, we must silence. This government has become the enemy of Mankind.

Death can no longer alter our path to Freedom. For our people, Death has been the only known exit from slavery and oppression. We must open others.

Our will to live must no longer supercede our will to fight, for our fighting will determine if our race shall live. To desire Freedom is not enough.

We must move from resistance to aggression, from revolt to revolution.

For every Orangeburge there must be 10 Detroits. For every Max Stanford and Huey Newton, there must be 10 dead racist cops. And for every Black Death there must be a Dien Bien Phu.

Brothers and sisters, and all oppressed people, you must prepare yourself both mentally and physically, for the major confrontation is yet to come. You must fight. It is the people who, in the final analysis, make and determine history, not leaders or systems. The laws to govern you must be made by you.

May the deaths of '68 signal the beginning of the end for this country. I do what I must out of love for my people. My will is to fight; resistance is not enough. Aggression is the order of the day.

NOTE TO AMERICA

America, if it takes my Death to organize my people to revolt against you, and to organize your jails to revolt against you, and to organize your troops to revolt against you, and to organize your children, your god, your poor, your country, and to organize Mankind to rejoice in your destruction and ruin, then here is my life! But my soul belongs to MY PEOPLE.

Lasime Tushinde Mbilashaka (We shall conquer without a doubt).

H. RAP BROWN.

From Revolt To Revolution

The New Proletariat: Nigger as class

In Sept. '67 (see Black Mask no. 8, Oct-Nov. '67) we carried an article on "The New Proletariat" which attempted to place the events of that summer into an historical context (the emergence of a new revolutionary class) and to begin the needed process of revolutionary coherence: that which could propel revolt to a level where theory and practice could be unified - in revolution (until that unification we will continue to have revolts but no revolution; ideology but no ideas).

The effort is even more difficult now because we are writing before the fact, and time is running out. The struggle has reached a point of advanced confrontation but the revolutionary process has only begun to unfold. No popular (as opposed to political) form of organization has yet emerged which can carry on that struggle. Those heroes who burned down Detroit have not yet found the organizational expression for that act. No counterpart to the assemblies of the Paris

Commune or the Soviets (Workers Councils) of the Russian experience have yet emerged. There has been some discussion of tactics - urban guerrilla - but none on the social forms which can make the revolutionary transformation: yet both are crucial - how to defeat "the man" and how to replace him. The bourgeois system is disintegrating and a vacuum is being created - but if we are not able to fill it, then they will be able to hold on (though only temporarily); and we will be dead.

The "Negro" revolution (civil rights) gave way to the "Black" revolution (nationalism) which must finally give way to the "Nigger" revolution the total expression of a new emerging class of dispossessed. There has always existed a dispossessed class (lumpen) but never has it occupied the center of social change being peripheral to the means of production. But that is changing as the system of production enters an automated and cybernetic stage and labor itself becomes obsolete. Now it is exactly these non-workers and automated ex-workers who are the most socially pivotal; it is how the system deals with them and their existence which shall determine its continuance; and conversely it is how we strengthen this consciousness that we succeed. We must expand the possibilities of this class and spread its social view: the question of "Nigger" transcends race and becomes one of class.

Obviously, at this point in America, that class is most clearly black (with some white drop-outs) but hopefully it will spread - Mexican-Americans, Puerto Ricans, and finally poor whites.

Malcolm X, of all the black revolutionists, was closest to this realization (that is why he was killed). He saw the need for "black" community and "black" organization (nationalism) and would not compromise this for synthetic alliances - but he also recognized the emergence of other revolutionary communities and would not deny them existence. But the concept of Black Power can in its search for "ideology" go in an opposite direction - it may ignore or reject an historical and class consciousness and may see "black" as pigmentation per se, rather than as pigmentation in context of white racist civilization, and that would be tragic: for a "Nigger" is a nigger first and black second. "When you live in the same kind of house, eat the same kind of slop, watch your children die when they're young or suffer due to no education when they're old - and somehow not feel as bad off as "the niggers" because your skin is white, then you are victims of one of the vilest, cruellest hoaxes ever perpetrated against a people." (Bob Analavage in the "Southern Patriot.")

In a recent speech, Stokely Carmichael hit on an extremely crucial point - he expressed what was most important but applied it in a totally backward way. "When you talk about alliances you recognize you form alliances with people who are trying to rebuild their culture, trying to rebuild their history, trying to rebuild their dignity, people who are fighting for their humanity." Here is the essence of revolutionary struggle; the struggle to be human. But then he says, "Poor white people are not fighting for their humanity, they're fighting for more money. There are a lot of poor white people in this country, you ain't seen none of them rebel yet (our emphasis) have you?" The answer is plain they have yet to see the possibility of being human - and to the degree that they do, so the revolution will emerge amongst them. They must first see they are "Niggers." They must define their own values and sub-culture which can struggle against the American plastic death; and when this consciousness has spread so too will the rebellions. Then Stokely's own answer as to why blacks rebel, becomes also our best answer: "Do you think its because its just poor jobs? Don't believe that junk the honky is running down. Its not poor jobs - its a question of people fighting for their humanity, for their humanity, FOR THEIR HUMANITY!" And there lies the revolution or its possibility. "UP AGAINST THE WALL MOTHER FUCKER!"

B. M.

Revolution as Being

The movements which proclaim as their goal revolution so far do no more than pronounce the syllables rev-o-lu-tion. A word may be rich in meanings and associations and thereby come to life; rev-o-lu-tion, however, remains a mere word. We ask, what is the content of that revolution? From what does it spring; towards what does it strive? The fate of our Being depends on the answers.

The question of what we are and what we would become - the question of Being - has not emerged. The rev-o-lu-tion instead carries forward the tortured edifice of the bourgeois life under the name of soc-ial-ism.

The movement springs from the oppression of the masses, but what is the content of that oppression? It is all too limited: economic exploitation and injustice. If this is the conception of the choking off of Being, then the goal towards which the movements strive is even more impoverished: a planned economy, social equality, freedom. It is not what is thus said, but what remains unsaid and unthought, that indicates the poverty of rev-o-lu-tion. The enemy is within as well as without; to think on Being and to Be revolutionary is to undertake to destroy a great deal of ourselves in the process. There is no distinction between the subjective and the objective in the revolutionary act. Being must everywhere be the basis of our thought and deed.

THE PROLETARIAN REVOLUTION IS THE SEXUAL REVOLUTION...
but why is the sexual revolution the proletarian revolution.?

The proletarian movement in the last analysis is distinguished from that of the working class; and even, in a fundamental sense, is hostile to it. It thus becomes all the more necessary to distinguish between the two when in our radical subculture proletarian is taken as synonymous with working class. The latter after all is only a category of political economy. As such it reveals a deep passivity when confronted not by the bourgeoisie (toward which the working class has always shown an egalitarian hostility) but by bourgeois civilization. The transformation of the working class into the proletariat takes place therefore not in the realm of political economy, but in the realm of Being. If our use of these terms differs somewhat from Marx's, it is still close to his early 1844 ideas.

The working class, by virtue of its exclusion from the more systematic structure of sublimation that constitute bourgeois society, has open to it the possibility of discovering Being. But the first stage of this discovery is the grasping and comprehending of that exclusion. This for Marx is, albeit implicitly, the transformation to the proletarian outlook. For us, however, more is required: the proletarian outlook is not simply the grasping of alienation, but the intuition of Being, or at least the possibility of Being. It is out of this soil that our Revolution grows.

For us, the object of trade union struggles is to destroy work: the object of ghetto struggles to destroy the ghettos; the object of student struggles to destroy the schools. And how is this to be done? Is it not Utopian? True, our aim is the destruction of reality, and thus we are Utopian - as Utopian as Detroit.

Our Revolution can begin, even in thought, only under conditions of the collapse of civilization. This condition is fulfilled today. The garbage heap affectionately called America by some, is disintegrating into its component piles of crap; it is a profound metaphor that the garbage workers refuse to collect the shit. In numerous union struggles Being has begun to leave traces of its existence: strikes are now transcending their ostensible demands; Being is everywhere at stake, yet it remains in shadow, concealed by economic demands. To bring it into the light, to struggle on behalf of Being - this is our goal. The Revolution is Sexuality trampling civilization.

JPM

The Theory of Synthesis and the Synthesis of Theory

(1)

The Left is dead, dreaming of a century that has passed it by. The movement for peace does not yet exist, since peace is only possible on the other side of the violent global struggle which is raging everywhere. The so called "Hippies" have staged their own funeral (Death of Hippie - devoted son of mass media, H/Ashbury SF, Oct 6). And the black struggle fuses its internal drive for liberation w/determination to organize and fight. No such equivalent will has yet manifested itself strongly among whites. But this is because the felt needs of the non-economic in life have never before been deeply experienced in white culture & are consequently not understood as inherently human demands on environment & now freed from labor by cybernetics the energies of creativity, love & social change are liberated from their 6,000 yr old repression. But man, the beast, does not recognize himself in his desires & fears them. for the moment he is still satisfied w/what is partial & incomplete...

But another force has also been set free by history - a subtle magnetism - for despite the failure of the movements which shout "peace, love & freedom," these desires are liberated in many of those who invoke them on the street. From the black struggle a black cultural focus has emerged as well as the repressed impulses of anger & hate which must complement the "hippies" liberation of our repressed impulse to love (Reich showed us this dialectic). The revolution occurs simultaneously on several levels (psychological & tactical): learning how to be revolutionary includes learning how to move in a revolutionary way.

(2)

We palefaces must become conscious of ourselves as part of the great rejected class - we are not White - but merely Light (light skinned brothers): because it is soul & not pigmentation that defines the sides in this struggle & what is necessary now for the Black community as much as the potentially revolutionary Lights, is the fusion of what is a still fragmented revolutionary movement into the cohesive force which will free us all: the growing militantism of the so called "New Left" must not be separated from the social-sexual content of the "hippies" or from the armed Black cadres. & likewise Black self-defense & guerrilla struggle need to be united w/emerging revolutionary Lights in a common recognition of the need to destroy the state (real political liberation, the end of politics), as well as abolition of bourgeois commodity values (real economic liberation, the end of scarcity economics) & the abolition of bourgeois social-sexual mores (real cultural liberation, the end of repression).

(3)

We are thru being assimilated: we will no longer make objects/our Art is Life/our medium revolution/& in a world based on repression our only message is Liberation. Our function is to make the Left hip & to make the "Hippies" left/to bring the body & mind back together/the unification of social consciousness & body consciousness/the creation of the Total Man.

A. H.

Totalist
P.O. box 698, Stuyvesant sta., N.Y., N.Y. 10009

"The Panther does not attack the Lion but together they kill the Hyena."

SECTION TWO

BLACK MASK
LEAFLETS

WE PROPOSE A CULTURE EXCHANGE
(garbage for garbage)

AMERICA TURNS THE WORLD INTO GARBAGE
IT TURNS ITS GHETTOS INTO GARBAGE
IT TURNS VIETNAM INTO GARBAGE

IN THE NAME OF UNIVERSAL PRINCIPLES (DEMOCRACY, HUMAN RIGHTS)
IN THE NAME OF THE FATHERLAND (COLIE DOGS, NEW ENGLAND CHURCHES)
IN THE NAME OF MAN   IN THE NAME OF ART
                    IN THE NAME OF MONEY

AMERICA TAKES
ALL THAT IS EDIBLE, EXCHANGEABLE, INVESTABLE
AND LEAVES THE REST

THE WORLD IS OUR GARBAGE, WE SHALL NOT WANT. WE LIE DOWN IN GREEN
    PASTURES. THE REST LIE DOWN IN GARBAGE

AND WE PLAY AS WE MAKE OUR GARBAGE
BEETHOVEN BACH MOZART SHAKESPEARE
TO COVER THE SOUND OF OUR GARBAGE MAKING

AND WE EXCLUDE THE GARBAGE FROM OUR PALACES OF CULTURE
AND WE WILL NOT ALLOW IT TO MARRY OUR DAUGHTER
AND WE WILL NOT NEGOTIATE WITH IT OR LET IT TAKE OUR SHIPS

BUT WE ARE FACED WITH A REVOLT OF THE GARBAGE

A CULTURAL REVOLUTION
GARBAGE FERTILIZES
DISCOVERS ITSELF

AND WE OF THE LOWER EAST SIDE HAVE DECIDED TO BRING
THIS CULTURAL REVOLUTION TO LINCOLN CENTER — IN BAGS
IS NOT LINCOLN CENTER WHERE IT BELONGS?

ASSEMBLE TO COLLECT GARBAGE ➡   5PM FEBRUARY 12 at
MARCH TO LINCOLN CENTER   (9th Street between C and D)
        BE AT LINCOLN CENTER BY 8:30PM FOR THE GARBAGE PLANTING C)

Brothers:

The assault against the black community in N.Y. has begun. They are attempting to divide in order to conquer. We in the white community must stand with our black brothers. The work of "provocateurs" and police agents has produced another frame-up (the Roy Wilkins murder plot) — to take the light off the real enemy — the "oppression" of life.

The labor movement should remember well the arrests and murders of union organizers (agitators) during the early 1900's (when they still had some revolutionary tendency) in an attempt to crush the real demands of the workers. Not by co-incidence do they now use the same laws, "criminal anarchy" and "syndicalism" in order to crush the black liberation struggle — they must not succeed.

Black Mask

Bulletin

By now everyone is aware of what happened in Tompkins Sq. Park on May 30 and the events which followed, yet not everyone is aware of the situation which has been created since.

The evening of the police assault on the park celebrants (which resulted in the arrest of 36 people and the hospitalisation of 3, one seriously) a large segment of the community went to the criminal courts bldg. (100 Center St.) to show solidarity for those arrested and out of concern for their fate. We were among those who arrived that evening, and after milling about with the others, decided to form a picket line protesting the police brutality (signs were made on the spot with poster-boards someone had had the presence of mind to bring). At this point a large segment of those "hippies" present made their opposition to our action known. They argued naively that we were making the situation worse by "protesting" and expressed the false hope that things would go better for those inside if we desist from our plan. We in turn explained that these people were victims of an unwarranted attack and that this was not an isolated case of brutality but a common experience for most ghetto dwellers (though new for them) engendered by a system of general oppression which exists and that this must be clearly understood before it can be stopped. At which point we were accused by Paul Krassner (editor, the Realist) of being "fascists — the same as the cops". Therefore those who protest the brutality are the same as those who perpetrate the brutality; an extreme perversion of both truth and language, which seems to have become common in the events which followed.

The next evening, Wednesday, an open meeting was held at the "Forum" to discuss what had happened in the park and what could be done. When we arrived the meeting was underway and it seems that Captain Fink of the 9th precinct had been speaking and was now taking questions from the floor to several of which he responded: "what happened was a mistake" (if it was a mistake, who did they mean to hit?) and that "the police weren't perfect" etc. At which point we interjected the opinion that nothing could be solved by speaking to the cops but that the meeting should be for members of the community so that they could decide and that this should include the Puerto Rican and Negro inhabitants of the lower east-side — that by speaking to the cops we gained nothing, but by speaking to our brothers we gain all. At which point a lot of cross-yelling began, some hostile, which resulted in Fink leaving and along with him those "reformers" who were only interested in smoothing things out with the police but not in examining the reasons behind what happened and how it could be prevented in the future. We were once again singled-out as "trouble makers" and though many people supported our position and the meeting continued, resulting in a committee being elected with a representative from each section of the ghetto; hippie, Puerto Rican, and black. We were later painted, by those who left early, as a "purely destructive force" and made to seem, somehow, the cause of the trouble which in fact had been started by the police. If our pleas for unity between the whole community, including the Puerto Ricans, had been heeded the tension which developed between them and the hippies the following night might have been avoided. Are we not all oppressed? Therefore let us unite.

We attempted to give coherence to the situation and place it in a revolutionary perspective but were accused of "seeking blood" and of trying to "exploit and create violence".

<u>VIOLENCE EXISTS</u> — <u>WE</u> DID NOT CREATE IT
<u>GHETTOS EXIST</u> — <u>WE</u> DO NOT PROFIT FROM THEM
<u>MEN ARE SUPPRESSED</u> — <u>WE</u> DO NOT SUPPRESS THEM

The local establishment and its media were looking for a scapegoat: and we were it. We have been singled out because we speak the truth, and "the truth is revolutionary". Those who have a stake in the system cannot blame the system. We can.

Black Mask

BLACK MASK
P.O. Box 512
Cooper Station
New York, N.Y.

BROTHERS, SISTERS, COMRADES & FRIENDS

You have noticed by now that BLACK MASK is no longer arriving — the last issue being #10 (April-May '68) — The reason is a direct result of our theory — The movement must be <u>real</u> or it will not be. Now the call is INTO THE STREETS...

The result has been more than a cessation of the publication of BLACK MASK, but also the resulting court hassles produced by our actions. The group which has transcended BLACK MASK, namely UP AGAINST THE WALL/MOTHERFUCKERS, is facing 48 criminal charges with penalties ranging from 10 days to 10 years. Money is an absolute necessity to fight the courts as well as to continue the struggle on all levels.

I myself am facing, in Boston, a 10 year sentence arising out of the issue of Self-Defense, and I go to trial Oct. 7, 1968. Money for this case is needed NOW.

Fraternally,
Editor, BLACK MASK
Ben Morea

UP AGAINST THE WALL MOTHERFUCKER
341 E. 10th St.
New York, N.Y.

SECTION THREE

UAW/MF

THE *FREE PRESS* REPORT

News distortion continues daily in the press's coverage of foreign news, particularly the war in Vietnam. There, according to United Press International, the most wildly inaccurate and widely used of the wire services, the Marines advance backwards while the Viet Cong retreats forward, the Marines capture while the Cong kidnaps, the Marines execute while the Cong murders. The Marines did not abandon Khe San, they moved away on search and destroy missions, three Marine transports shot down by Cong artillery became the worst air crash in aviation history and the present Cong offensive on Saigon is being conducted only for some inscrutable Oriental conception of propaganda.

This summer the hip community has been the subject of the same sort of treatment. Except for some sympathetic editorials from the Globe, the hippies have been vilified as degenerate, dirty, a public nuisance.

No serious attempt has been made to understand their philosophies or their decision to fight for the Common. No report has been made on the harassment, attacks and poisonings inflicted upon them by members of the outside community.

The press has been content to base its reportage of events on the Common on statements issued, with small regard to truth, by the Boston police. The Record American has been the most classically biased and vindictive of the local papers.

Matters came to a head last week when, after the arrests of more than one hundred members of the free community for violations of the Common curfew, Ben Morea of the Up Against the Wall Motherfuckers SDS chapter of New York was reported as having stabbed a recuperating Vietnam war veteran.

Morea, the New England Resistance and SDS members called a press conference the afternoon of July 24 to argue Morea's innocence and protest the actions of the press in general and the Record American in particular.

What followed was a labored exercise in non-communication. Not one line was reported in the press the following day. The Free Press presents a slightly condensed transcript of the entire proceedings in order for the people of Boston to understand better the Battle of the Common and why the established media is both unwilling and incapable of reporting events truthfully.

Up Against the Wall Mother Fucker

Press Conference report in the *Free Press.*

Photos by *Richard Wellins*

Ben Morea: The existence of our community represents both an alternative to the present system and a means for its destruction. The hip community poses a way of living rather than simply a way of surviving. On the one hand it rejects old middle-class values, especially that of the consumer life, on the other hand it makes possible a fuller and more complete life. Out of that emerges a revolutionary culture.

Consequently, the media which is the propaggator of those old values is obligated to distort the hippie and his actions. At the same time, that which it cannot distort it must assimilate. They take the superficialities of our dress and appearance and ignore our revolutionary values. They sell our fashions and ignore our soul. Because the hippie is a threat, the mere fact of his living becomes a crime; similarly, the black man is a criminal just for being black. Hippies are niggers. Like the black man, they are insulted, harrassed, beaten and arrested.

The Arlington Incident is a case in point, only one in many. The press and media distortions helped spread and deepen fear of the hip community, The curfew was imposed both because of this fear, and more importantly, as a means of preventing us from having the space to assemble as a community. Businessmen, in particular, took action against us on Beacon Hill and elsewhere because we refused to buy their bullshit. Those of us driven form the Common were then arrested and driven from the street. Forced to go in to the Arlington St. Church, we were then isolated from our own community and left open to attack.

This attack is itself the product of the media's campaign to misrepresent us and alienate the rest of the community from us. Specifically, in this last incident, we found ourselves pitted against young military men equally oppressed and exploited by the same society we fight. For example, there are two kinds of pigs at the Common: civilian and military. The society fear the exploited coming to the free community at the Common; the military knows that should the soldiers join us they would no longer be tools of their own oppression.

At the same time, when we find ourselves attacked, we must and will defend ourselves regardless of how we feel about the attacked. The black community has realized this for a long time; we now must realize this. As far as we are concerned, those in the black community like Huey Newton who defend themselves against assault be it by civilians or the cops are totally justified. Similarly we assert the right to defend both ourselves and our community. In order to build a revolutionary community, we understand that we will have to fight.

As a beginning, we announce a program of education and direct action against the Record American, the paper especially vicious and brutal toward our community.

Globe: I was wondering who you see yourselves as representative of, what group? In making this statement, I understand you represent the so-called hippie community?

Ben Morea: I don't represent the hippie community. I'm a part of it. I want to clarify one thing. The hippie community is not a regional community. There is no such thing as a Boston hippie community, a New York hippie community, a San Francisco hippie community. There is one hip community and it spreads from one end of this country to another . . .

WEEI: Where are you from?

Ben Morea: I'm from New York.

WEEI: Why are you in Boston?

Ben Morea: I moved to Boston. I intend to stay here.

WEEI: How long have you been here?

Ben Morea: Oh, about a week.

WEEI: You say you moved to Boston, did you take up residence? Do you work? What attracted you to Boston?

Ben Morea: The hip community here was under a kind of pressure that existed in other places around the country and I felt that the pressure should be resisted

every place . . . Therefore I feel strongly that other members of the hip community all over the country have a need to defend the existence of the Boston hip community.

WEEI: Would you say you came here more to join the community or to fight the Establishment?

Ben Morea: They're the same thing.

WEEI: No.

Ben Morea: Oh, yes they are.

WEEI: The same as what?

Ben Morea: We feel that the existence of the hip community itself is fighting the Establishment.

WEEI: In other words, then you set up the hip community as a kind of violent, oppressive . . . They certainly don't seem passive. They represent the overthow of the Establishment.

Ben Morea: There are many means of overthrow. I don't reject violence. At the same time, I don't see violence as a possibility for building what we want.

Christian Science Monitor: How do you plan on and how do you describe the concept of love and acceptance and honesty in reference to the hippie community that is known to be apolitical? How do you feel that this has to be reoriented? regarding what you just said for self-defense?

Ben Morea: Well I don't find the idea of self-defense or even violence contrary to the idea of love . . . I don't feel that that community is specifically a love community, but is a total community. And in order to be total, we understand that that means all elements of living. We don't reject one element or the other. What we would want, the ideals we want, specifically is to create the kind of life that doesn't need violence. I don't like violence, but at the same time we recognize that to be full men, we don't have a need to reject any part of living.

If we are attacked, we don't submit to attack. That is what the press would like to make believe the hip community does . . . The hip community is not the pacifist movement that exists in America. It's a different thing. The hip community is a full community, a culture, a way of life, a way of existing. It's not just a tactic or a means, or another form of pacifism. Many people in the hip community are pacific and would nót use violence. But there are others in the hip community who feel that we must defend those values that we pose as an alternative to American values.

WEEI: Would you come in and set up your way of life in the midst of another way of life and take it over? Physically take over land that other people had used for other purposes?

Ben Morea: American society took over land from the Indians.

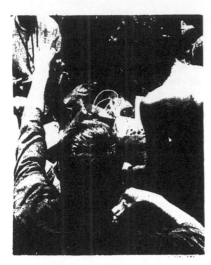

WEEI: Well, you're not an Indian.

Ben Morea: We are all Indians. All of us are Indians. We are the return of the Indians.

WEEI: You are the return of the Indians?

Ben Morea: That's right. You destroyed those people.

WEEI: I didn't destroy those people.

Ben Morea: You destroyed those people with your culture which is the sickest culture that ever existed. Understand? You destroyed those people physically, culturally, and in every way you could. We who grew up in your society now know what you did, and we feel more affinity with them than with you. We are their descendants, we're not your descendants.

WEEI: How old are you?

Ben Morea: 26

WEEI: You're older than I am. So it's your culture, not mine. (The reporter exits.)

Christian Science Monitor: In the beginning of the summer there was an influx of hippies, and they said that there would be an even larger one. A lot of these kids have left, and there were a number of leaders who were more or less speaking for the hippie. Have you been in contact with them . . . those who have been in contact with the police and more or less spoken to the authorities in Boston, and in some way gotten the Establishment off the hippie's back? . . .

Ben Morea: First of all there's a false impression that has to be cleared up. Number one, nobody came here. No one came here and started trouble. There's trouble here. There's trouble every place in America. Except there's two kinds of trouble, visible and invisible. A day or so after I arrived eight kids were arrested in the morning for doing nothing but sitting on the grass. That is trouble, understand?

The people who speak to the mayor, to the police, were unable to prevent that from happening. The only way that we can prevent that from happening is making it clear that we're not going to allow members of our community to taken off one by one. If they're going to drive us out, they're going to have to tackle all of us, not just one or two of us. Those people who talked to the mayor and the police are not interested in the individual members of the hip community. They're only interested in saving a kind of false relationship. They don't care that eight people were arrested and told to leave town immediately as long as there seemed to be a pacific relationship between the Establishment and the hip community. But the minute that people got together and said these eight people are our brothers and we're going to stay with them on the Common and not allow them to be driven out of town, then all of a sudden the press finds that there's trouble. They didn't find trouble in the morning . . .

Herald Traveler: Ben, if I may again speak of defense, you will defend yourselves, am I correct?

Ben Morea: That's correct.

Herald Traveler: In what particular way? Weapons?

Ben Morea: I'll defend in response to the attack. If we're attacked verbally, we defend ourselves verbally. If we're attacked culturally, we defend ourselves culturally. If we're attacked violently with open hands, we'll respond violently with open hands. If we're attacked with weapons, we'll defend ourselves with weapons.

Herald Traveler: May I assume from that statement about weapons that there is a supply of weapons available for your use? . . .

Ben Morea: Our energy is itself a weapon.

Herald Traveler: You don't mean anything physical do you? Guns or anything like that? I just want to make that clear.

Ben Morea: If you shoot at me then what would be my equal response?

Herald Traveler: You would respond in kind?

Ben Morea: That's all I said.

Herald Traveler: You don't have an arsenal or anything?

Ben Morea: No. Nobody has an arsenal. Nobody is interested in any arsenal. The police have the arsenal.

Christian Science Monitor: This might be a rather naive question, but I was wondering if you are so committed to fighting the Establishment, is there anything in America that you directly respect? Do you believe that the laws regarding drug abuse — for example, this has been one of the concerns of the hippie community, drug abuse and drug use — do you make separations? Do you feel that there has to be a re-education of knowing how to respect laws in a way that they're not hypocritical?

Ben Morea: We reject drug abuse. We consider the police to be the abuser of drugs. We consider the Establishment to be the abuser of drugs because they abuse us because of our use of drugs. Drugs are part of our community. I think a very important part . . . I personally think that those drugs that allow people to grow rather than allow people to remain without growing. And I separate drugs into several categories . . . In terms of categories there are repressants, those which — it's a very ironic thing, you can see this in the ghettoes and you can see in other places, that certain drugs are used for several reasons. Number one, to repress your own awareness. When the possibilities of living are denied you, you turn into yourself, which is very close to dying. You use certain drugs to help you do that, and I generally reject that. I find that where hip communities are under constant harassment by the Establishment, the turn is more and more to drugs which are repressants . . .

Just like the ghettoes turn to heroin, so that happens in hip communities when they find that possibilities of living, when they find their freedom curtailed, and they withdraw into that kind of repressant thing. The communities where the hippy can grow, where he can define his life styles, and be allowed to do that, the drug use is usually in terms of expansion drugs, like marijuana, hashish, and LSD or whatever, and it's up to the individual in the hip community to use what he feels is necessary for his existence. I would not be for imposing restrictions within our own community. What people use is up to them, but at the same time I feel that us building the kind of environment that we want would limit that . . .

The people on the Common are being driven off that and there are people in other parts of the city who are withdrawing to their part of the city because there is a general fear of all to coming together and trying to build a total kind of existence because of the pressure from the straight community.

Christian Science Monitor: Could you explain why New York has become such a source of corruption for the hippie community?

Ben Morea: New York is a source of corruption. The Establishment built New York. I didn't build New York. When they force me into a little box, I begin to look like the box. So people in New York reflect the kind of environment that is around them, so that the hippie community there tends to be under different pressure than in other places. But in New York, you know, like Boston and other parts, there is more similarities than difference.

Globe: What is your total aim? A non-violent community? Isn't that correct?

Ben Morea: You mean in terms of projection? Absolutely. The difference is this. The Indians also had a non-violent community. They didn't have police. There was little fighting between themselves. They had a non-violent community but when you attacked them, they would respond violently.

Herald Traveler: But they had extensive tribal wars. American history verifies that.

Motherfucker: I think that you'd better re-read that.

Herald Traveler: They didn't have any tribal wars or anything among themselves? . . .

Ben Morea: All I'm trying to say is that we believe in a total way of living. Let me explain this to you. It might seem a little metaphysical. There is an energy which is living, life. If you block that energy, it's going to knock you down. If you allow the energy to pass through you, good. Now we have that energy. If you come in front of me and try to prevent me from living, to prevent me from flowing, then I'm going to knock you down. If you just allow me to live, and allow my energy to pass, then good.

The dichotomy is always made between non-violence and violence and that's a false dichotomy. The dichotomy is between living and death. That's the dichotomy that we have to begin talking about, not non-violence and violence, living and death. Some kinds of violence are living, understand? Some kinds of violence are death. If your violence is because you desire to live and is only directed against people who would prevent you from living, then I don't consider that violence. I consider that living. If your violence, like the police violence and the military violence, is directed against others, killing others, that is violence because it's death.

That's the difference. I'm tired of hearing all this talk of violence and non-violence. We can talk about living and dying, and our community represents life as far as we're concerned, not death.

Your community represents death. You eat dead food. You live dead lives. You fuck dead women. Everything about you is dead. I'm not talking about you personally, but your community.

Resistance: You're welcome to change communities at any time.

Free Press: Can you tell us about some of the actions against the Record American you are taking?

SDS: I'll just relate it, tie it into something that went on similarly in Germany earlier this year, and that was the demonstrations against Springer. The constituency for change in West Germany began moving to a point this year where they began to understand the role of the media in Germany in their efforts to change, to reconstruct Germany, to rebuild a Germany that was a free one, that was open to people to live full lives, to live lives that they control, and decide the direction for themselves.

They began coming up against the press, one particular arm of the press that was very important in repressing their efforts and that was Springer. They found Springer behaving as an arm of an oligarchic network that was oppressing the people of West Germany . . . The social impact of the press has

been to confuse them as to the reality of the world, to disorient them, to stop them from taking action to reconstruct the world along humane lines. Specifically in Germany they found that the Springer press was confusing people about the nature of their work, their school system, and the nature of their political parties. That situation in Germany led to direct action assaults upon this arm of what was viewed as part of a fairly coherent oligarchic network . . .

In this country that situation is very closely paralleled by the Hearst press . . . The Hearst press has confused people of the role of their bosses, politicians, ward healers, local Mafia representatives, of their local police, their pigs who really oppress them. The Hearst press has told the people that these agents of the oligarchy are acting in their interests when in point of fact these agent are acting to keep them down. Specifically in Boston the Hearst press has told people that the police are their friends . . . They have told them that the military is doing good things such as making war on Vietnam. They have told the people that the system that employs them, the capitalist system that employs them, is in their interest. They have told the people that the police are their friends. They have also told them that black people are their enemies, that anti-war and anti-imperialist radicals are their enemies . . .

That in many ways, I think ought to be viewed essentially criminal in that it is making, trying and convicting innocent people, people working for liberation of crime, and turning the people of Boston against them. It is fair to say that the Hearst press in Boston had a very direct role in turning marines, similarly oppressed marines, to attack members of the hip community, that the Hearst press has a direct responsibility for the violence that has occurred, and that is criminal, that the perpetration of that violence is criminal, that the Record American has acted to turn the people of this city against each other to preserve the interests of the power rulers.

We encourage people to turn away from this wing of the press to other wings of the press that feel that sense of social responsibility to a greater depth, for instance, in Boston, the Boston Free Press is one that strikes many of us as acting on a sense of social responsibility to tell the truth . . . We will employ direct action to highlight that advocacy.

Resistance: One of the things that they did was to turn military men against the people like us. It was military men in that fracas. It's military men who were hurt. It was military men who were down there believing that we were their enemies . . . We feel sympathy for the military men, those Marines, who are being used by this government to fight the war over there. You see we have been setting up relationships with those men. Men are coming in to see us because they know that we are friendly to them. We understand their plight. We understand they're being used. But what is happening is that through the Record American and through some other papers the impression is being created that the hippies are the enemies of the soldiers . . .

What the Record American is doing is putting us all up against the wall . . . creating that atmosphere of hate which gets those Marines down there thinking that we are their enemies. So we're up against the wall and we have to defend ourselves.

Free Press: The American society is now a society that is hunting for its enemies everywhere. They are very frightened. They're very much in a position of not being liked or appreciated by anyone in the world because they're so oppressive throughout the world. The American society is truly a heavy burden on this planet, and because of that the Record American which operates as a competitive newspaper in Boston is willing to press anything which will find an enemy for a group of largely ignorant people and when you have any minority that can serve as its possible enemy — because if you print a story where you have one minority posed as an enemy of a larger number of people you sell a lot of papers — so the Record American has again and again acted totally irresponsibly as a newspaper and tried to make the majority of people believe that one of these minorities is their enemy.

Herald Traveler: The press conference has taken a turn here where it's apparently a direct attack on the Record American. I'm not from the Record American. I think that what you should do is get together with the Record American and have a press conference with them. I'm certainly not going to publish any of the remarks about the Record American.?

Ben Morea: It's not just the Record American.

Herald Traveler: What are the other papers?

Ben Morea: It's not just the other papers . . . All of the papers in America represent something that is in some way opposed to what we represent, that they are part of the Establishment that we lie outside of.

Herald Traveler: But Ben, you're calling a press conference as if you had a group of scientists and then you blast science. And we're sitting here gentlemenly enough . . .

Ben Morea: I just want to point out one thing. The soldiers and the incident . . .

Herald Traveler: I'd like to keep it on that basis.

Ben Morea: Now I hate to bring the press in again, but there were a lot of people in that attack. I'd say at least 20 people attacked a group of us which numbered about eight people. Out of that 20, only five or six were soldiers.

I mean the press has made believe that it was only an assault by military men because they'd like to push that image more . . . As far as I know the soldiers that were in the direct attack were not in a physically disadvantageous position. There were no wounded soldiers. That thing about a guy beingon crutches is nonsense. There was in fact a soldier on crutches who was in fact quite a distance away from the fight. He had two crutches when he came, but just before the fight startedhe decided he could walk on one crutch so he gave his crutch to someone else to use as a club which was swung against the back of a bystander there during the fight . . .

Herald Traveler: Now first of all, Ben. It could have to do with the reporter, who was down there and probably reported it that way. It wasn't the editor. The publisher wasn't there. You're making a wholesale charge about the paper.

Ben Morea: The editor is responsible. There is no paper who covered it at all who talked about the fact that somebody was attacked and defended themselves. All the newspapers created the image that we somehow hurt those soldiers, that we somehow stabbed these soldiers, that we somehow fought with these soldiers.

Herald Traveler: When did the press get there? What time did the fight break out?

Ben Morea: I don't know.

Herald Traveler: Some of these incidents that you speak of could have happened before the arrival of a newspaperman.

Ben Morea: They found out what happened. And they reported it only one way.

Herald Traveler: I wasn't there, I don't know.

Resistance: Why didn't you report that you weren't there and don't know? The press knows, that's their attitude.

Christian Science Monitor: How do you guarantee in your own efforts in the New England Resistance or the hippies in not becoming witchhunters, similar to the anti-Communists. I remember listening to many of the accusations that the hard-core anti-Communists did during the 50's and they made similar accusations about the press, too? . . .

Ben Morea: That is the most, WOW, I can hardly believe that. They are the witchhunters, we are the witches. Then you turn around and say how are we going to stop witchhunting. They are trying to burn us. That is the witchhunt, understand?

Christian Science Monitor: How do you differentiate between true self-defense and paranoia?

Ben Morea: I'll tell you what, if you attack me, see how paranoid I am . . .

Avatar: Can I say one thing. I'd like to point back a little bit to the consciousness of the past that you were speaking about earlier. I think the thing that the press has forgotten is that they are not consciously aware that everything they write is public opinion. This is their responsibility. They are acting as the mind of the people. They have to be very sure of just what they are doing because the actions that the police take depend on what the press says. If the press says this, then the people go call the police. Then the police have to react

on it. Indirectly, if some kids get beat up on the Common and get killed, the press started it and directly, sure, the cops are the ones swinging the clubs, but indirectly the press was the thought of it, and the idea was the public.

Ben Morea: That's partially true. There's a little more. It's not just the press, but all of American society that causes it really. I mean the press is only the vocalization of what is going on in America. There is something in American society that is afraid of life. And there is something in American society which we have rejected because of that. You know we have rejected that. Therefore, to save your own false illusions, you attack us. The press becomes the vocalization of that, the cops become the tool of that, and the courts become the carrying out of it, and these poor soldiers become somehow also the pawns of it.

But it's not just the press, it's not just the cops, it's not just the Marines, it's not just the straight people who attack. It's not. It's something in American society itself that is drastically sick. That's the cause of the problem. That's why we call ourselves a revolutionary community because we understand that death. We have rejected that death, and we don't want that death. And if you attack us, we are going to give it back to you.

Free Press: Can I ask a question of the press? There's a thing on the Common now called the Common Newsletter. Has anyone from the Globe, the Herald Traveler or the Record American bothered to pick it up and read it and find out what is bothering the hip community and bothered to report on it?

Globe and Herald Traveler: I haven't seen a copy of it . . . First I've heard of it.

Free Press: Well, don't you think that if your papers are going to write about the Common and editorialize that they should take the trouble to send a reporter down to be aware of these things. Surely it's the press' duty . . .

Herald Traveler: But, of course, you must realize that this is just one phase of so much news that is coming in to our newspaper city room during the course of 24 hours. First of all, they sent me down to Lynn yesterday on a $138,000 hold-up. I trust I gave the facts as I saw them as a reporter.

Ben Morea: Well, then, give the facts of these incidents . . .

Avatar: Within the system of a newspaper you can write anything and never know whether it is going to be published.

Herald Traveler: That's right. In other words, I can go back and write a story but that doesn't guarantee that it's going to be in.

Avatar: Right, because some guy back there wants to make money and sell papers. And so he doesn't care . . .

Herald Traveler: It's not that at all. It's simply that I'm not writing it correctly. The grammar wasn't right

Ben Morea: Let's get a few things clear in your head or notes or whatever it is. Number one, the curfew is totally illegal and unconstitutional.

Herald Traveler: Ok, I want to get this now. The curfew is totally illegal and unconstitutional, right?

Ben Morea: It was imposed against us as a community to drive us out, that when we were driven from the Common into the neighboring streets, then we were arrested in those streets which was illegal and unconstitutional, and when we were driven from those streets and reassembled at a church we were attacked. As a result of the press distortions, as a result of the police attack on us, then the rest of the people stand around and figure that you're a criminal since the police are attacking you, so let's go attack you also. That we were attacked there, get it clear in those damn papers that we were attacked, that we defended ourselves, that it was not a matter of a fight . . .

Resistance: Do you think that statement would ever make one of the Boston Newspapers?

Herald Traveler: I know the word bullshit won't get in.

Ben Morea: No, that statement of what actually happened. Did it ever get in that often when somebody is arrested that if he has had some sort of altercation with the police he is beaten by the police on the way to the station.

Herald Traveler: I'd have to have that proved?

Ben Morea: Well I want to tell you something. When I was attacked, when the police grabbed me, I told the police that six fellows attacked me, one with a lead pipe, one with a board, and several with bricks, that they attacked me and I defended myself as an individual. They were not interested in those six people who attacked me, they didn't look at them, look for them, they grabbed me. I want that to be understood.

Herald Traveler: First of all, we're doing a job. My assignment today is to come down here and cover this press conference. This is an attack on the press.

Ben Morea: Well, cover that statement.

Herald Traveler: Do you know for a fact that the police did not seek out those six?

Ben Morea: They categorically refused. I pointed out one of the individuals and I said I want that man do you understand taken for assaulting me, they refused. When one of them was brought to the police station, I said that man had a brick. I want him arrested and they refused. I was in the cell, do you understand?

Herald Traveler: Ok, I'll quote you on that.

Free Press: Is it true that the Record American has better police contacts than other papers?

Herald Traveler: I'm not in a position to say that. I work for the Herald Traveler, and have for 25 years on that paper. I have many friends on the Record American and I don't think they have any more a pipeline so-called than we do.

Free Press: Other reporters in Boston that I've talked with seem to be in general agreement that the Record American is capable of getting crime stories much more quickly from the police department than the other papers.

Herald Traveler: Is there a Record American reporter here?

Resistance: NO.

Globe: Was he invited?

Resistance: NO.

Motherfucker: Can I make a statement about you feeling you have to defend the press being down here covering a news conference and then you hear, you know, of what you conceive of as malicious statements against the press?

Herald Traveler: Wait a minute now. Don't put words in my mouth, buddy. I didn't say malicious statements. I said a charge has been leveled against the press.

Motherfucker: There is no analysis behind what the idea of media is, how it functions, and how it operates. Now

it is not always a case of individual culpability. It's not saying that you working for the Herald Traveler distort the news because you want to nail somebody against the wall. And you don't think it that way. That is not what is meant by consciousness. There is a concept behind mass media now, that basically number one, it is Establishment. It belongs to the system. It is part of the system and it conceives of itself as basically operating within the values of that system as a whole.

Herald Traveler: What you should have here, I think, are the publishers. That's who you should have here.

Motherfucker: The point is that you are here as a representative of the publisher. You work for the publisher as his representative. Now unfortunately there are two sides of being his representative. One is doing his bidding, and sometimes it's taking the other side of his bidding which may be verbal attacks on the press in general.

Herald Traveler: Wait a minute. You said his bidding. In my 25 years experience as a newspaper reporter on the Herald Traveler I have never been bidden or ordered by my publisher to do anything.

Motherfucker: Have you been told to go out on a story?

Herald Traveler: I have been assigned by an editor who is not the publisher to go on a story.

Motherfucker: I believe there is a chain of command, isn't that correct?

Herald Traveler: What, is the publisher notified every time a news story breaks?

Motherfucker: Is the president notified every time a soldier fires a weapon? No, all right? But there's a general chain of command. When the publisher says to the editor cover the news, it is known that generally there are certain types of news items that publishers say "are too hot too handle."

Herald Traveler: Specifically, what publisher are you talking about?

Resistance: There is a sign in the Record American building right outside the editorial room signed by William Randolph Hearst and there is a sentence in that to the effect, report the news that only nice people want to read, the nice American great middle-class, that's almost a direct quote.

Herald Traveler: I've never seen that.

Resistance: It's on the third floor, right outside the door.

Motherfucker: What it comes down to is not only the idea of upholding social values but the whole psychological way that the press works on people, the way the media does . . . There are certain important news stories no matter how they are distorted that carry certain values to people . . . What happens in a newspaper is that they are chopped up . . . On a page right next to something like a continuation of the Cleveland story there is a gigantic advertisement right next to it. There is a psychological tendency to have an equalizing effect .

Herald Traveler: But you're talking about make-up now.

Motherfucker: No. It's a concept that underlines our whole criticism of media, that there is an equalizing tendency to say that toothpaste that brightens your teeth is as important as people being shot in the streets. Not that one is more important than the other, not that it drags down in importance the people being shot in the streets, or bolsters the importance of toothpaste, it just equalizes them, whether it's at a high level or a low level. It's just a psychological thing that happens and it's very important when you consider what the press or media does to a whole society in terms of how it operates on their consciousness.

Herald Traveler: You're criticizing the press for what it hasn't accomplished. Our circulation is not that great. We had to go out of business with one paper . .

Resistance: That's a matter of economics . . .

Herald Traveler: As Ben pointed out just a while ago, that society is sick. Now is he crediting the press with being responsible for all this? Can't society be sick without a press?

Ben Morea: The point is that a sick society needs a certain kind of press. It creates that press, a sick press, and that's what happens . . .

Black People

What about that bad short you saw last week on Frelinghuysen, or those stoves and refrigerators, record players, shotguns, in Sears, Bambergers, Klein's, Hahnes', Chase, and the smaller joosh enterprises? What about that bad jewelry, on Washington Street, and those couple of shops on Springfield? You know how to get it, you can get it, no money down, no money never, money don't grow on trees no way, only whitey's got it, makes it with a machine, to control you, you can't steal nothing from a white man, he's already stole it, he owes you anything you want, even his life. All the stores will open if you will say the magic words. The magic words are: Up against the wall motherfucker this is a stick up! Or: Smash the window at night (these are magic actions) smash the windows daytime, anytime, together, let's smash the window drag the shit from in there. No money down. No time to pay. Just take what you want what you need. Dance up and down the streets, turn all the music up, run through the streets with music, beautiful radios on Market Street, they are brought here especially for you. Our brothers are moving all over, smashing at jellywhite faces. We must make our own World, man, our own world, and we can not do this unless the white man is dead. Let's get together and kill him my man, lets get to gather the fruits of the sun, let's make a world we want black children to grow and learn in do not let your children when they grow look in your face and curse you by pitying your tomish ways.

— LeRoi Jones (Amiri Baraka)

SECTION FOUR

UAW/MF

MAGAZINE

WE ARE ALL UNDESiRABLES

The existence of our community represents an alternative to the present system and a means for its destruction. The hip community poses a way of living rather than simply a way of surviving. On the one hand it rejects all middle class values, especially that of consumer life; on the other hand it makes possible a fuller and more complete life. Out of that emerges a revolutionary culture. Consequently the media which is the proprietor of those old values is obligated to distort the "hippy" and his actions. At the same time that which it cannot distort it must assimilate. They take the superficialities of dress and appearance and ignore our revolutionary values. They sell our fashions and ignore our soul.

Consequently, because the hippy is a threat, the mere fact of his living becomes a crime. Similarly the black man is a criminal for being black. Hippies are niggers. Like the black man they are insulted, harassed, beaten and arrested.

The Arlington incident is a case in point, only one of many. The press and media distortion help spread and deepen the fear of the hip community. The curfew was imposed both because of this fear and more importantly as a means for preventing us from having the space to assemble as a community. Businessmen in particular took action against us on Beacon Hill and elsewhere because we refused to buy their bullshit. Those of us driven from the common were then arrested and driven from the streets. Forced to go to the Arlington St. Church, we were then isolated from our community and left open to attack. This attack is itself the product of the media campaign to misrepresent us and alienate the rest of the community from us. Specifically in this last incident we found ourselves pitted against young military men equally oppressed and exploited by the same society we fight. For example, there are two kinds of pigs on the common: civilian and military. The society fears the exploited coming to the free community of the commons; the military knows that should the soldiers join us they would no longer be tools of their own oppression.

At the same time, when we find ourselves attacked we must and will defend ourselves regardless of how we feel about the attackers. The black community has realized this for a long time. We now must realize this. As far as we're concerned, those in the black community like Huey Newton who defend themselves against assault be it by civilians or by cops are totally justified. Similarly we assert the right to defend both ourselves and our community. In order to build a revolutionary community we understand that we will have to fight.

"The algerian fidai (death volunteer), unlike the anarchist made famous in literature, does not take dope ..."

F.Fanon

when the vast body moves thru battlefield streets
it walks on many legs
hungry cells and angry bellies
guts of anger/blood of anger
anger in the one fantastic throat that cries:
"Now! Now this body sees, this body feels
this body knows and aches, this body
will suffer to be chained no more!"
and when the vast body moves thru battlefield streets
the great buildings tremble...

                             henry/uaw-mf

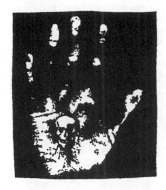

Columbia University, as an institution owned and run by the same interests that run corporate America, can never create an education directed to the overthrow of those interests. A revolutionary movement wishing to educate revolutionaries cannot come to terms with Columbia. But the strike, although it speaks the rhetoric of revolution, cannot bring itself to admit what must be its ultimate goal: so its formulations are often confused and unconvincing.

A revolt at Columbia would have to cut Columbia's ties to the ruling corporate structures of America. This means taking power from the trustees and money interests that support Columbia. It cannot then be expected that Columbia will be supported by the money it is in revolt against. Without that money there is no Columbia. but the strike leadership denies that it wants to destroy Columbia.

Example of resulting contradiction:

question of amnesty/one does not ask the authority one is revolting against to legitimize ones' revolt, unless one is unsure whether one is revolting or not. Amnesty was presented as both a tactical (we cannot negotiate with the university with punishment over our heads) and revolutionary demand (we will not accept anything short of amnesty because there is no legitimate authority to punish us). Which way is it baby, you can't have both?

If the rhetoric of revolution is to be believed, then the demands for reform of Columbia are tactical. One urges ones demands to expose, to force polarizing crisis. The strike becomes a source of energy that will burn thru the dry straw of academic life: its guiding principle - disrespect & bad taste!

Kick the professor in the gut (if he stands in yr way).

Slash the Rembrandt (if the threat will stop the pigs).

Put their chinese porcelains on the barricade (Headline: Pig smashes art treasures).

Rifle thru their files, stealing anything you can use to embarrass or blackmail them.

Smoke the president's cigars - they're from Havana anyway.

We must destroy something old & dying, in order to make room for what is new & beautiful. And our only demand must be: ALL POWER TO THE COLUMBIA COMMUNES!

MY UTOPIA IS AN ENVIRONMENT THAT WORKS SO WELL WE CAN RUN WILD IN IT

UNTIL OUR MOST FANTASTIC DEMANDS ARE MET, FANTASY WILL BE AT WAR WITH SOCIETY. SOCIETY WILL ATTEMPT THE SUPPRESSION OF FANTASY, BUT FANTASY WILL SPRING UP AGAIN AND AGAIN, INFECTING THE YOUTH, WAGING URBAN GUERRILLA WARFARE, SABOTAGING THE SMOOTH FUNCTIONING OF BUREAUCRACIES, WAYLAYING THE TYPIST ON HER WAY TO THE WATER-COOLER, KIDNAPPING THE EXECUTIVE BETWEEN OFFICE AND HOME, CREEPING INTO THE BEDROOMS OF RESPECTABLE FAMILIES, HIDING IN THE CHAMBERS OF HIGH OFFICE, GRADUALLY TIGHTENING ITS CONTROL, EVENTUALLY EMERGING INTO THE STREETS, WAGING PITCHED BATTLES AND WINNING (ITS VICTORY IS INEVITABLE).

WE ARE THE VANGUARD OF FANTASY.

WHERE WE LIVE IS LIBERATED TERRITORY IN WHICH FANTASY MOVES ABOUT FREELY AT ALL HOURS OF THE DAY, FROM WHICH IT MOUNTS ITS ATTACKS ON OCCUPIED TERRITORY.

EACH DAY BRING NEW AREAS UNDER OUR CONTROL.

EACH DAY A NEW VICTORY IS REPORTED.

EACH DAY FANTASY DISCOVERS NEW FORMS OF ORGANIZATION.

EACH DAY IT FURTHER CONSOLIDATES ITS CONTROL, HAS LESS TO FEAR, CAN AFFORD TO SPEND MORE TIME IN SELF DISCOVERY...

EVEN IN THE MIDST OF BATTLES IT PLANS THE CITIES OF THE FUTURE.

WE ARE FULL OF OPTIMISM.

WE ARE THE FUTURE.

The poverty of present forms of organization consists in their limitations — men work study & sometimes love & die together — but they do not any longer know how to LIVE together - to share the wholeness of their lives . . . But despite them, the forces which bring men together constantly assume new forms.

In the present struggle forms of organization must soon come into being that are appropriate to the changed conditions that are the real content of our times. Not least of all they must be forms that are tenacious enough to resist repression; forms which can grow secretly, learning to manifest themselves in a large variety of ways, lest their mode of operation be co-opted by the opposition, or they be simply smashed.

*   *   *

The affinity group has qualities of both the pre-organized form & the post-organized form. & it is because of these qualities that it will fulfil our needs. In fact it is absolutely necessary that we transcend all bourgeois forms of organization - including the so-called "revolutionary" party. The political revolution can only serve to change the form in which hierarchical power is distributed— while our task must be to form a new cultural whole in which social control is returned to the people — a social revolution that will change the content of everyday life, as well as its structure.

For us socialism & its forms of hierarchical organization must be abolished along w/bourgeois parliaments & democracies, so that no mere political form be allowed to impose itself on the content of a much more complex & multifarious life.

*   *   *

The affinity group is the seed/germ/essence of organization. It is coming together out of mutual Need or Desire. Cohesive historical groups united out of the shared necessities of the struggle for survival, while dreaming of the possibility of love. For man's nature is not bounded by necessity alone - Desire appears in all its forms & man desires to desire - he seeks to fulfil himself on every level of his complex life. & it is in this psychological sense that the affinity group is a pre-organizational force, it represents the drive out of which organization is formed/& in so far as it fulfils men's desires it becomes the post-revolutionary form, the organization of satisfaction. But the immediate need is for mutual struggle, for a new technological organization of resources, a new distribution of wealth, re-establishment of ecological principles (to re-create harmony in a disrupted nature), to create a whole new complex of free relations between people, that can satisfy all our complex needs for change & our consuming desire to be new & to be whole.

*   *   *

What we have called the de-structuring of organization is not merely a proposal to create a particular structure for this period of pre-revolutionary activity, but is designed to show the relation of all organization to its base & to insure control at the bottom by forcing all structures back on the affinity groups that are at their core.

In the pre-revolutionary period affinity groups must assemble to project a revolutionary consciousness & to develop forms for particular struggles. In the revolutionary period itself, they will emerge as armed cadres at the centers of conflict. & in the post-revolutionary period they become models for the new everyday life.

In this way the organization transcends the historical problem of centralism vs. de-centralism, by making all structures a dynamic inter-relation of centralist & de-centralized elements: affinity groups coalesce to form large organizations/simultaneously engaging in public struggles for consciousness & maintaining an active underground.

In so-called "primitive" unitary societies the affinity group attempts to balance a complexity so thorough that it approaches totality. But the division of labor that arises from the struggle for survival causes a fragmentation & un-evenness in the distribution of material as well as psychological & cultural wealth. But now with the development of an automated-cybernated technology the material problem can be substantially solved — freeing man from labor as well as scarcity — liberating his time, his energy & his Desire, simultaneously, generating the possibility for an entirely new coherence, of becoming whole, Total.

Presidents & financiers who oppress us
are as empty as their lives,
Their money is as worthless
as the products they shit,
And all the objects of their culture
are as meaningless as their flags.

All their concepts of the universe
are as vacuous as their TV tubes,
And even our insignificant lives
are a judgment against theirs.
For they speak only the language of oppression
and we have presented the vision of a new life.

Remember that the men who control your life
create the terms of existence,
And to escape reality in your sleep
is your final consolation.

But we who struggle with our lives
plant the seeds for future rebellion:
Our knowledge of ourselves
is our greatest conquest,
And any glimpse they get of our world
gives them nightmares.

They understand only half the truth,
can't see the two forks
of the serpent's one tongue,
And all their passionately held ideologies
are nothing but the memory
of <u>our</u> past struggles.

a motherfucker translation of the Buddhaa

THE BEST ORGANIZERS WILL JOIN US AT THE TIPS OF THE IMAGINATION

What time is it 1:
Here in the faltering wings of the future
there is no food in the crash pads tonite
in the crashing pads we create to house our community
to house ourselves, to house our affinity groups
here in the anarchy, the pure communism we are living
in the loving last period before social illumination
in the time before the revolution that will splatter
our bodies on fields we haven't seen from bowling green
to chicago lakes to bay area bruises to wheatfields
in kansas to jackson deaths and birmingham riots to
atlanter

What time is it 2:
Here, in the misty vanguard of having and needing
and desire without pennies, money being antique property
here, where the cave ends and a new reality begins
beings without state pronounce Lenin's mantra:
        there is no freedom
        until there is no state
        until there is no state
        there is no freedom
from state or state and revolution

Program:
flower-cong running naked in the streets
dangling erections in the face of tourists
fucking each other, provoking bloody flood of
police sadism (Inspec. fink, forgetting his public image, sweating
over a nite stick, grinding it into the vagina of some young hippiess)

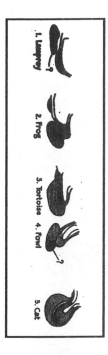

Sermon:
all that is of value in amerika lies with us.
we are its custodians. now we are a harassed remnant.
in the future that remnant will unravel into long threads
with which to weave new values into the world

the police use their clubs like tampax to stop the menstrual
flood of revolution. the only thing that will stop the flood
will be the birth of revolution - which will be bloody.

Final:
There is the man and there is us.
These are the forces that are against us:
the large part of white plastic amerika that can see life
only in terms of material accumulation (every aspect of
humanity becomes commodity), the supporters of the law of
property, those that are bound by only one dimension
of life. The anti-life bureaucracy is preparing itself for
total repression - cultural genocide. We must find the forms
that express our sense of communal struggle! Forms of life
to express our opposition to the anti-forms of anti-life.

UP AGAINST THE WALL MOTHERFUCKER

SECTION FIVE

UAW/MF
INTERNATIONAL
WEREWOLF CONSPIRACY

LEAFLETS & ARTICLES

POWER TO THE COMMUNES

Columbia University, as an institution owned and run by the same interests that run corporate America can never support an education directed to the overthrow of those interests. A revolutionary movement wishing to educate revolutionaries can not come to terms with Columbia. Ultimately its goal must be to destroy Columbia. But the strike, although it speaks the rhetoric of revolution, can not bring itself to admit what must be its ultimate goal. So its formulations are sometimes confused and unconvincing.

A revolt at Columbia would have to cut Columbia's ties to the ruling corporate structures of America. This means taking power from the trustees and money interests that support Columbia. It can not then be expected that Columbia will be supported by the money it is in revolt against. Without that money there is no Columbia. But the strike leadership denies that it wants to destroy Columbia.

(Example of resulting contradiction: question of amnesty: one does not ask the authority one is revolting against to legitimize ones revolt unless one is unsure whether one is revolting or not. Amnesty was presented during the strike both as tactical (we can not negotiate with the university with the punishment over our head) and as more than tactical (we can not accept anything but amnesty because there is no legitimate authority around to punish us). Which is it.

If the rhetoric of revolution is to be believed, then the demands for reform of Columbia are tactical. One urges ones demands to expose, to force polarizing crises. The strike becomes a source of energy that will burn through the dry straw of academic life: in one door of the campus and out another). Its guiding principle: disrespect, bad taste.

Kick the professor in the stomach (if he stands in your way)

Slash the Rembrandt (if the threat of slashing it will deter the police one must be willing to make the threat real.

Pile the chinese porcelain camel on the barricade (Headline: policeman's axe smashes art treasure.)

Rifle through the files. Smoke the president's cigars.

A Little Treatise on Dying

The student is shit. He is the privileged person in an underprivileged world of suffering, but only because he does not recognize his own boredom as a form of imprisonment, of torture. He is not only deadened to reality, he is also deprived of the consciousness of his own suffering. He accepts himself as 'normal', but it is only the normality of his repression that makes him like the rest of society.

The student movement is blind to itself: it does not understand the forces that push it into action, it cannot connect its struggle with its own life. (The issue is clearly not credit for Cleaver's course, or racist hiring practices — the issue is not the issue — and Cleaver for Janitor is no solution.) The student movement seeks 'demands' everywhere, but because students cannot see the absurdity of their own lives and their own imprisonment, they cannot begin to imagine what the struggle is for.

Students in France, Japan, and especially Mexico, are struggling and dying in the streets in the real fight for liberation . . . and revealing the poverty of our own movement and the terrible artificiality of our 'struggles'.

The real struggle will be easy to recognize because it will cut thru all the bullshit in which we are trapped. It knows its objectives. Its tactics are clear. It moves with confidence. It is struggling to WIN.

We begin by killing the enemy within us, within the hearts and minds of those with whom we would share our bodies and our lives. We come together in small bands with those we have learned to trust, preparing for the long struggle with the enormous power of the institutions that repress us.

An Act of Destruction is an Act of Liberation

The function of the student movement is not to make demands on the university, but to destroy the existence of the 'student' as a social role and as a character structure. YOU MUST DESTROY THE STUDENT WITHIN YOU. For only then can the struggle begin against the institutions and masters which have trained us for the submission and slavery in which we now participate. Our goal is not to win concessions, but to kill our masters and create a life which is worth living . . . and IN AMERIKA LIFE IS THE ONE DEMAND THAT CAN'T BE FILLED.

international werewolf conspiracy

"Practice without theory
remains unfulfilled;
but theory without practice
fulfils only itself."
                    (Jack the Ripper)

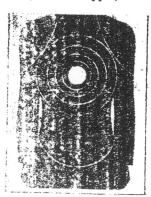

Everywhere in the world the
old reality reigns ———
socialism/capitalism, the
illusion of opposition
divides the world . . .
And here, for us, the same
reality is everywhere
reproduced ——— the new left
vs. the old left ———
the PL/"New Worker" split:
the front and the back
but everywhere the same
counterfeit coin ——— stamped:BOURGEOIS REALITY

If the revolution is anything it is TOTAL
new ideas, new forms of organization, and above all NEW LIFE

The need is apparent, only fear stands between us and UTOPIA

"And if you don't believe in lead,
you're already dead." (Huey P. Newton)

UP AGAINST THE WALL MOTHERFUCK

APPENDICITIS:

Affinity groups exist within revolutionary organization, but cannot be organized. A few people come together out of the kind of friendship and trust that maximizes security on every level. Relying on each other, the individuals in an affinity group increase their potential for action and decrease the dangers of isolation and/or infiltration. The necessity for these relationships should be obvious at this stage of our struggle . . . Affinity groups are not cliques — they are created for the purposes of security and activity, not simply for the exclusion of other people. Affinity groups are formed for both specific and general purposes, and will find both the needs and means for working together with other affinity groups within their own collectives and locals.

UP AGAINST THE WALL MOTHER FUCKER
Lower East Side, N.Y.

"Hip revolutionaries have the Power to inspire FEAR." ——— Sorel

We are the ultimate Horror Show . . . Hideous Hair & Dangerous Drugs . . . Armed Love striking terror into the vacant hearts of the plastic Mother & pig-faced Father.

The future of our struggle is the future of fear, FEAR!! The fear of free love, fear of not working, fear of youth . . . We drink the magic potion and become the spectre that haunts Amerika. We are the WEREWOLVES baying at the moon and tearing at the fat. Fangs sharpened, Claws dripping. We are not afraid. We create fear. (the Pig wanders from his sty . . . and the wolves descend).

"Where do they come from?" Who knows. "What do they want?" They won't say. But the moon knows. And the WEREWOLVES know. And the fat frightened giant gulps tranquilizers while his children grow hair and fangs and leave home to run with the wolves.

"We have nothing to fear but fear itself," he said.

"But what about the wolves?" she said, anxiously.

A small town filled with comfortable merchants and their well-fed wives, lies twinkling in the valley as the clouds drift peacefully across the night sky. In the distance a wolf howls, and another one answers, and another, and another, and soon the night is filled with the roar of howling wolves. The sounds merge into a chaotic chorus as the wolves gather together under the fullness of the moon . . . Lights go on all over town. Gentlemen in pajamas rush to their windows, unable to sleep because of the horrifying sound carried by the night wind. Women in curlers clutch the blankets close around themselves as the shadowy, howling shapes move through the streets.

When morning comes, there is silence. The wolves have gone away, have moved on in their mysterious way . . . Their stomachs sag with the weight of a satisfying feast, and their fangs drip with the fresh blood of their victims.THE CHILDREN OF THE TOWN RUN BESIDE THEM.

One of the wolves stops long enough to say. "Survival."

Another one answers him, "REVOLUTION!"

The worst fear is the fear of the unknown, and we are the unknown . . . THE UNKOWN . . . WE ARE WEREWOLVES! International Werewolf Conspiracy Up Against the Wall/Motherfuckers

THE MYTH KILLER

We must develop our own standard of beauty

The Hip Community exists because we have abandoned the institutions of this so-called society:

home/family, school, job, army etc.

We are all runaways.

Wherever we are the Hip Community exists:

the street, the pad, the park, the subways — all night, the pawnshops, the coffee houses, Gem's spa — the place doesn't matter.

Considering the many levels and the tremendous mobility of the hip community, in order to survive, and survival is what we are concerned with, there must be link ups. There must be focal points in each city where our community can base itself . . . .

The rest of his childhood he spent in hiding . . . he was an unpopular kid.

What's real to us is dinner in our stomachs

What's real to us is music we can dance to

What's real to us are all those things that are necessary for a living community, for a fighting community: karate classes, bail and defence funds, Anti Pig Militia, communal meals, crashpads, communes . .

WHAT'S REAL TO US IS SPACE TO SURVIVE,

What's real to us is to feel, to fuck, to dance, to sing, to take dope, to jump up and down, shaggy haired, fang-toothed with everything hanging out.

To survive in Amerika as a total human being is revolutionary.

Hip is living, really living, and to live in Amerika

IS A CRIME PUNISHABLE BY DEATH.

As the threat of our community grows repression becomes greater and the need for survival space becomes more urgent.

We can not allow the man to define us or our space.

Everywhere we turn Bullshit Amerika has been defining what we do and who we are. We have allowed the media, the record companies, the psychedelic merchandisers and the suburban imitators to tell us what the "Hip Revolution" is all about — NO MORE

We must now launch a total assault on every form of oppression that seeks to limit our existence and our possibilities.

Controlling our lives means creating total freedom

BY ANY MEANS NECESSARY.

We must create the hip revolutionary community

We must destroy Amerika because it has nothing to offer us but death.

The INTERNATIONAL WEREWOLF CONSPIRACY is the Hip Revolutionary Community in Action. Insanely hungry for the chance to discover how to live, and rabid for the blood and guts of the honkies and pigs who infect everything they see with the plague of living death.

WEREWOLVES OF THE WORLD, JOIN THE FEAST

International Werewolf Conspiracy

Up Against the Wall/MOTHERFUCKERS
Al Paredon Hijo de Puta
Berkeley Commune
Boston Freemen
Church of the New Reality (Southwest)
October 15 Movement
Flower Cong
and You

AFFINITY GROUP = STREET GANG WITH AN ANALYSIS

'Ideas can create life-and-death situations, but a man can really only fight and die for himself and for the lives of his friends.'

— Chief Joseph

In the present struggle, forms of organization must come into being that are appropriate to the changed conditions that are the real content of our times. These must be forms that are tenacious enough to resist repression; forms which can grow secretly, learning to manifest themselves in a large variety of ways, lest their mode of operation be co-opted by the opposition, or they simply be smashed.

The Affinity Group is the seed/germ/essence of organization. It is coming-together out of mutual Need or Desire: cohesive historical groups unite out of the shared necessities of the struggle for survival, while dreaming of the possibility of love.

In the pre-revolutionary period affinity groups must assemble to project a revolutionary consciousness and to develop forms for particular struggles. In the revolutionary period itself they will emerge as armed cadres at the centers of conflict, and in the post-revolutionary period suggest forms for the new everyday life.

Mass demonstrations succeed in two ways: they bring predominate levels of consciousness into the streets and make visible the quantity of active alienation in our society . . . and they sometimes transcend the issue of 'demonstration' to become mass actions. As mass demonstrations they fail to advance the nature and forms of our struggle . . . as mass actions (whether against cops or against property) they begin to define the direction and the reality of what our struggle must become. 'Riots' or rebellions are the highest form of mass action as it (1) liberates goods and geographical areas, and (2) engages the occupying forces (PIGS) in battle. This form, too, has advantages and limitations, and it is in response to both of these that people are discovering the tactical/theoretical possibilities of working together in small intimate groups. The prospects for the future are clear in at least one respect: the Man and his Pigs are learning 'crowd control' and they are escalating their response to all masses of people who take it upon themselves to behave in violation of this society's 'law and order'. Our preparations for advancing the struggle must always take into account the abilities and tendencies of the enemy. Mass demonstrations and community rebellions will continue to serve particular needs in many situations. . . . But in the general sense of ongoing struggle it is necessary that we begin to act in that manner which is most favorable to our means and to our goals . . . THE SMALL GROUP EXECUTING 'SMALL' ACTIONS IN CONCERT WITH OTHER SMALL GROUPS/'SMALL' ACTIONS WILL CREATE A WIDESPREAD CLIMATE OF STRUGGLE WITHIN WHICH ALL FORMS OF REBELLION CAN COME TOGETHER AND FORGE THE FINAL FORM: REVOLUTION . . .

Already we have the small group response. . . . Columbia's Communes, Berkeley's Revolutionary Gangs, France's Committees of Action, and others so far only known by their actions (Cleveland). In the months to come these groups and the many others which will be forming face two kinds of absolute necessity as they seek to create the possibility of real community:

1. Internal development and security. Each group will continue to create its own sense of identity through the conscious synthesis of theory/practice, and each group will apply this identity to the existing reality in the most effective manner.

2. External relationships with similar groups. We must begin to set up those forms of communication and mutual awareness that can allow for greater mobility and greater response to more-than-local crises. This means that we will have to create a network of affinity groups (both within existing communities and between those communities).

This network of 'Federation' must be characterized by a structural looseness which guarantees the identity and self-determination of each affinity group, as well as an organizational reality which allows maximum concerted actions directed toward total revolution.

The concept of the affinity group in no way denies the validity of mass actions, rather this idea increases the revolutionary possibilities of those actions. The active minority is able, because it is theoretically more conscious and better prepared tactically, to light the first fuse and to make the first breakthroughs. But that's all. The others can follow or not follow. . . . The active minority plays the role of permanent fermenting agent, encouraging/inspiring action without claiming to lead . . . In certain objective situations . . . with the help of the active minority . . . spontaneity finds its place in the social movement. It is spontaneity which permits the thrust forward, and not the slogans or directives of "leaders". The affinity group is the source of both spontaneity and new forms of struggle/life.

[Editors Note: This text also appeared on the reverse of "Into the Streets" with just the first three paragraphs and the last paragraph signed by the Boston Freemen and Up Against the Wall/Motherfuckers]

opposites flowing
merging
into one
life energy
moving into
perpetual revolution

Another Carnival of Left Politics

It seems the respectable left organizations (YSA, PLP, SDS, PFP, ISC) never tire of providing entertainment for the bourgeoisie — and worse, keep trying to rechannel any really radical energies back into their bullshit forms. Their self-styled 'revolutionary attitudes, based supposedly on Marxism (antique 19th century ideology), certainly aren't reflected in their lifestyles — just ask one for a buck or a fuck. . . . And now that Huey is convicted what will they do??? Sadly, we all know, they'll have another rally, they'll picket death row, they'll march on the courthouse, they'll shift from their tv armchairs to auditorium armchairs; while they sit righteously clukking like hens, disapproving of the 'terrorists and provocateurs' who are taking care of business. And in the absence of any relevant politics they make false separations and throw around labels. Well, who are the saboteurs and the terrorists??? We are. All of us who will sabotage the foundations of amerika's fucked up life; all of us who strike terror in the heart of the bourgeois honkies and all their armchair bookquoting jive-ass honky leftists/white collar radicals who are the VD of the revolution.

And if there's a panther or french student on the stage talking at them, they go home feeling radical, as if revolution were a disease you could get by association. . . . The only thing a liberal or honky leftist is good for is to throw between me and the pig/or to jack up for lunch money. And when the people on the streets realize it they'll run the bastards back to their tv sets.

At the same time we must understand the role these organizations have played. PFP has rallied elements of the white community to the 'support' of the besieged Panthers/ but the time for support is over, not to speak of the time to stop playing with bourgeois forms of electoral politics. And YSA rallies have provided a focus for street energies, but rallies and pickets won't stop the racist pig oppressor.

What we have to realize is that these early levels of struggle have been transcended by the development of the struggle itself. Chicago reveals a higher form of street event and the bomb on Telegraph reveals another, while Cleveland's ambush offers an altogether higher plain, moving us towards real (not metaphorical) guerrilla struggle . . . But at our present stage of development the issue is not whether we should take to the streets, finding some form of mass expression, RATHER than engage in clandestine activity. There is no separation in the revolutionary movement. Every act is assimilated into the struggle, if it furthers the revolt. . . . We must be flexible to rally one day and bomb the next. And we must find new forms for massing and moving in the street at the same time as we create alternative modes of actions when street action is impossible.

And in France we saw that the worker-student alliance didn't come about because the workers responded to traditional left forms of organization, but because they saw the students and street people moving the struggle to a real level of confrontation in the streets. And in a post-industrial world, what have the traditional leftists to offer workers who know that their work is meaningless.

traditional leftists to offer workers who know that their work is meaningless. Certainly not another dose of the protestant work ethic. They still can't understand it/ but in 1919 when they were struggling for higher wages and better working conditions DADA was in the streets calling for total unemployment and the new man. And today we offer automation, cybernation and free love on the streets.

But beyond these considerations the movement must understand the real reasons for its actions. We do not take to the streets because we want free speech or free assembly (those are liberal demands)/nor do we take to the streets in 'support' of Chicago or Paris, or anywhere or anyone else (including 'support' of Huey). We have our own struggle. We are fighting for ourselves/for our community/for our very lives. The issue is not something other than ourselves/we are the issue. It is the liberation of our lives that we are fighting for/to liberate ourselves from tight-assed bourgeois life, and it is our experience of the boredom and misery of amerikan life that drives us to destroy it anywhere it confronts us.

Berkeley Commune

Up Against the Wall/Motherfucker

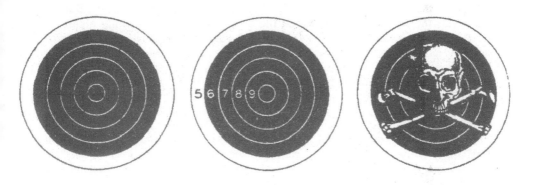

Acid-Armed Consciousness

Acid-armed consciousness
We are the balance of cosmic energy
we are the freaks of an unknown space/time
we are the sys of the revolution
Destroying-creating everywhere a new reality exploding into an environment
An environment that must be transformed
Our gargantuan strength spiraling through the unreality of this country
Tearing away the past and present
We are the future
We are the eye of the revolution
We are a tribal culture — a community of families armed with drugs/magic/guns
Our weapons are our lives flowing together living together merging constantly
We are one. We are one.
We are the eye of the revolution.

40,000 blacks and longhair brothers of the boogie movement (in california alone) are securely locked in jail for what are seemingly only drug busts. But the man fears the real threat of out total life change that drugs are only a part of. Freaks in other cultures have always found ways to turn on and trip naturally since men had minds to explore and explode. Yet LSD is truly a product of this culture's technology and the trip can be as plastic as the system that made reproducible the internal serotinin turn-on. Just as we can liberate the cybernetic experience to free men from work and the machines that bind their bodies, we can expand the psychedelic experience beyond the glorified plastic mechanism that still plugs in some minds. Even the most 'freed' freaks can use acid and be used, to be overwhelmed instead of to overwhelm, to be terrified when we should be terrifying! Only when we simultaneously see our magic drugs as an ecstatic revolutionary implement, and feel our bodies as the cellular macrocosm and galactic microcosm will our spiral/life energy destroy everything dead as it races over the planet leaving us alive spinning at the pineal eye.

Blown minds of screaming-singing-beaded stoned armed-feathered Future-people are only the sparks of a revolutionary explosion and evolutionary planetary regeneration. Neon Nirvanas finally overload their circuits — Watts pull out the plug and sets the country on its own inextinguishable electrical fire a we snake dance thru our world trailed by a smokescreen of reefer.

SELF-DEFENSE

SELF-DEFENSE IS PREPARATION AGAINST ATTACK.

SELF-DEFENSE IS THE RESPONSE TO ANY ATTACK.

SELF-DEFENSE IS THE REPRISAL FOR AN ATTACK.

WE MUST DEFINE OURSELVES FOR OURSELVES IN THE
LANGUAGE AND GESTURES OF OUR OWN DISCOVERIES

WE MUST LEARN TO RECOGNISE EACH OTHER AND TO KNOW
THAT ANYONE WHO IS NOT WITH US IS THE ENEMY

WE MUST LEARN TO FIGHT AS WELL AS SEEK TO LOVE

WE MUST TAKE UP THE GUN AS WELL AS THE JOINT

WE MUST DEFEND OUR COMMUNITY AND OUR OWN HUMANITY.

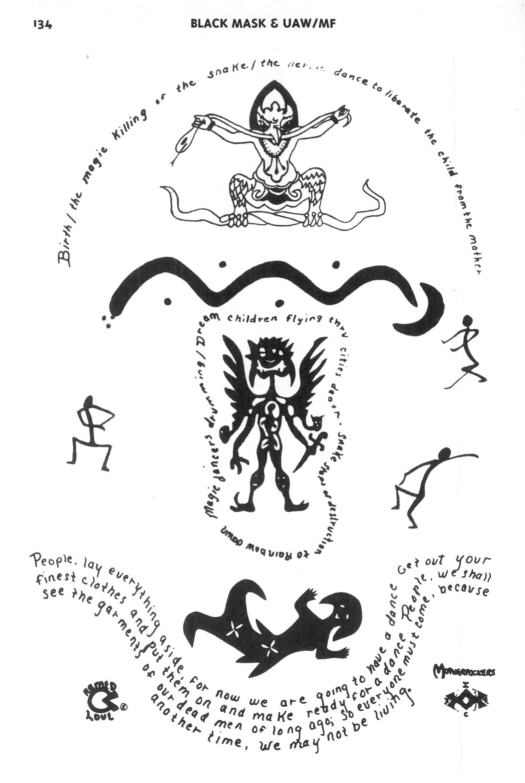

TO LIVE ONE MUST LOVE
     TO LOVE ONE MUST SURVIVE
          TO SURVIVE ONE MUST FIGHT!

                              —MOTHERFUCKERS— W.W I. C.

Revolution in dreams
Revolution in books
Revolution in cars
Revolution in advertising

but everywhere <u>repression</u>.

repressed living as the
expression of everyday life

And your biggest enemy is your ASS.

pick it up
let it move
Make it happen

is anything else in nature straight = NO =
where the fuck did it come from?
From your fucking heads.

Can you sleep with Che under dorm regulations?
Will Aretha Franklin sing the 6th International?
Can you MOVE!

Street music:
Tactical Pig Symphony vs. the Invisible Street Band / banned / ban
                                      BAMN
                                      By Any Means Necessary

And despite everything the man can do--we will survive, we will grow,
          and dig it--we will win!
Make It Happen.

The Bossman (No-Balls/man) sees the threat of the Street whore
luring "his" young from the programmed possibility of their
existence into the only <u>real</u> possibility of existence -- luring
the worker's sons from factory smoke to the smoke of the burning
factories--And now "living" is possible for everyone.

"Poor Dad, too bad, Momma hung you in the closet and I'm feelin'
     so sad."
So pick his pockets
Take his watch
Steal his gold teeth----

And Support you local Revolution -- MAKE IT HAPPEN

Revolution in Dreams

Revolution in dreams
Revolution in books
Revolution in cars
Revolution in advertising

but everywhere repression

repressed living as the
expression of everyday life

And your biggest enemy is your ASS

pick it up
let it move

make it happen

is anything else in nature straight = NO =
where the fuck did it come from?
From your fucking heads.

Can you sleep with Che under dorm regulations?
Will Aretha Franklin sing the 6th International?
Can you MOVE!

Street music:
Tactical Pig Symphony vs. the Invisible Street Band/banned/ban
        BAMN
        By Any Means Necessary

And despite everything the man can do — we will survive, we will grow and dig it
— we will win!

Make it happen.

The Bossman (No-Balls/man) sees the threat of the Street whore luring 'his'
young from the programmed possibility of their existence into the only real
possibility of existence — luring the worker's sons from factory smoke to the
smoke of the burning factories — And now 'living' is possible for everyone.

'Poor Dad, too bad, Momma hung you in the closet and I'm feelin' so sad.'

So pick his pockets
Take his watch
Steal his gold teeth —

And support your local Revolution — MAKE IT HAPPEN

Summer Solstice, New Mexico

Summer Solstice . . . New Mexico

Trying to examine — understand point reached by Hip People. Consciousness—Reality . . . with brothers from the Hog Farm family . . . the Armed Love, Motherfuckers tribe . . . and heads from all over the country . . . recognition of ourselves as a people grows, but family—tribe—commune attendance still small . . . The Be-in again replayed and transposed . . . The tribal gathering still a reality to work for . . . the gathering of those family—tribes— communes which are the foundation of the Hip Nation.

Woodstock . . . only two families, Hog Farm and Motherfuckers present within the overall family of all hip people . . .tribal gathering seems further from reality but closer to existence.

The so-called 'Movement' left bankrupt, unable to move — flow — influence . . . find themselves lost in a sea of people — drugs . . . the two families at home with their people . . . The Hog Farm feeds — cares for its people-free consciousness in its present future state. While Motherfuckers liberate for and supply their people's needs. Hundreds of tents and sleeping bags distributed free by psychedelic bandits . . . taken from straight business stands where they were selling for $20, and distributed free . . . stands where profits were labeled 'Love' knocked over and goods given freely and lovingly by stoned psychedelic warriors . . . 1,000 hits of sacred acid distributed while Krishna fakers sing against drugs . . . 2,000 years of repression emerged as bald-headed faggots.

There is no 'movement' other than the body-soul movement of our people. Fuck the so-called left. New division-unity, seen-understood . . . ying-yang life-death. The division between left-right is false . . . the division is between life and death. Hip-Life consciousness must replace political death consciousness as revolutionary alternative and tribal social consciousness must replace left wing party consciousness as revolutionary hope. The real criticism must be total . . . western death trip must be opposed on all levels . . . the western so-called 'revolutionary attempt cannot succeed to overthrow the death root of the western totality since it is a product of the same partial thought pattern. Western civilisation itself has to be destroyed . . . and new life-forms created . . . the struggle is as total as life itself.

Tribal-social pattern the beginning of the 'real' alternative. Patterns of life emerge as patterns of growth. The hip tribal nation forms as the eventual replacement of amerikan all-government. The hip tribe as cultural-social-political totality in unity-federation . . . life as the social form. Those of our people-who have passed beyond being drop-outs . . . the negative of a negative . . . to being free men with new life patterns-can but only build that new nation and new life . . . as new men, poets, dope-magicians, healers, warriors, creators; whatever we are-needed. Those of our people who have had the 'vision' will not be stopped, killed. Those for whom the century old oppression has loosened cannot be fooled again. The circle of oppression-death has been broken. A new circle is being formed; one which reverses the total anti-life motion of our recent history.

What has been lost must be re-found . . . what is refound must be strengthened. Evolution within revolution. Are the western 'politicians' so blind as to think there is 'a' revolution? There is a history of revolutions . . . a process . . . a coming and going. Cybernetic-technological nomads . . . space age indians . . . psychedelic freak bandits . . . what was not before is now . . . what is now will not be again.

Never has the revolutionary possibility been so complete . . . to be in touch with the cosmic, to re-create environment, to re-find life is a monumental project compared to the mere overthrow of a government . . . we challenge the total oppression of man of which until now the revolution has been part. We challenge the revolution itself. Power to no one. Life to everyone.

Sun Eagle

(Armed-Love-Motherfucker tribe)

Hip Survival Bulletin

Armed Love ◄───► Love Armed

Spring has come, hip communities blossom under the warm sun, but warmth brings the pig heat. Every night our people are being busted for hanging out on St. Marx Place. Three Motherfuckers busted — one for being a runaway — two for helping their brother.

They use riot police to stop us from hanging out, from talking and playing our music, from living on our streets.

If the people in the street were more together, the man couldn't hassle us so much. If the people on the street were more concerned about their brothers, they wouldn't allow the man to bust so often. There are ways to stop the pig from busting. Don't let any brother be taken so easily — grab, circle, distract the pig, don't make it easy for him!

BOSTON: The pigs are cracking down on our brothers and sisters! Hassling and busting for not wearing shoes. Using old laws (1894) about blocking public passageways — two or more people standing on a sidewalk. The pigs have put a curfew on the commons.

HIP PEOPLE must be out of the park by ten o'clock. They tried to fuck us up last year. They tried to stop us growing together. They're trying to do it again.

Communication among the Hip Community throughout amerika is necessary. Send all information and [illegible] to the Motherfuckers: East Side Survival Organization, P.O. 512, Cooper Station, New York, N.Y. 10003

CHAPTER REPORT ON THE S.D.S.
REGIONAL COUNCIL OF MARCH 10

A MOLOTOV COCKTAIL
IS A BOTTLE FILLED WITH
THREE PARTS KEROSENE
AND ONE PART MOTOR OIL
IT IS CAPPED
AND WRAPPED
WITH COTTON
SOAKED WITH GASOLINE

TO USE —
LIGHT COTTON
THROW BOTTLE

FIRE AND EXPLOSION OCCUR
ON IMPACT WITH TARGET

A "WHITE RADICAL"
IS THREE PARTS BULLSHIT
AND ONE PART HESITATION.

IT IS NOT REVOLUTIONARY
AND SHOULD NOT BE
STOCKPILED
AT THIS TIME

respectfully submitted

UP AGAINST THE WALL

MOTHER FUCKER

Fillmore Free Theater Leaflets:

October 22, 1968. Tonight the people return this theater to themselves. Originally our demands were modest, one night a week free for the people of the FREE community. Bill Graham (who within the archaic legal frames was technically in control of the theater) refused our demands. Now we take what is ours anyway. The theater now belongs to the people, including Bill Graham.
The seats belong to the people. . . .
Once we asked, now we take. . . .
The Fillmore is no longer onemans, but everymans. . . .
WE MUST PRESERVE THIS LIBERATED TERRITORY! NOW

               STAY   FREE   FREE
                    STAY   FREE   FREE
     STAY   STAY   FREE   FREE
          STAY STAY FREE   FREE   FREE
                              *

FROM THE LIBERATED ZONE
FREE PRESS
BULLETIN

We have been in the free zone for only a short time — already are experiencing the real problems of freedom —
— Should we stay till we get exactly what we want or leave and come back next Wednesday when we have the same alternative —
— How do we create out of the sea of free elements that flows through the theater — a community — an order that is liberating.
— What tools do we need to create ourselves as a community — a printing press, a microphone? What?
— What do we do with our freedom (some people become frustrated). Some people look for leaders. It is easy being an audience.
— Enough rhetoric.
Let's talk to each other — meet in groups — rap — form larger groups — relate our individual arts to the whole. TIME TO PUT THE SHIT TOGETHER NOW!
STAY RAP STAY RAP STAY RAP STAY RAP STAY RAP STAY

                              *

Bill Graham has said that next Wednesday we can have a community meeting. This must be the start of a free theater for a free community.
The community needs free space. It needs it to survive, grow freaky, breathe, expand, love, struggle, turn on — Bill Graham, hippie entrepreneur, who has made money from our music, but claims the right to his property for himself — may tonight have been a little liberated. Or he may not. Next Wednesday will tell.

FREE THE THEATER
FREE BILL GRAHAM
FREE EVERYTHING
ONE NIGHT A WEEK OR THE SKY'S THE LIMIT

SECTION SIX

UAW/MF

ROLLING STONE REPORT

Fillmore East vs. The East Village
— The Full Report by Paul Nelson

The contretemps between Bill Graham and the New York Motherfuckers contingent has been simmering and boiling toward bloody violence for weeks. A full report on the background, the foreground and all the attendant emotions that brought the rock people and the revolution people into confrontation, as prepared by Rolling Stone's New York bureau, follows.

NEW YORK — In retrospect the stormy and sometimes violent 10-week battle between Bill Graham's Fillmore East and the "revolutionary" Motherfuckers-led segment of New York's East Village hip community was a clash between two styles of life — two philosophies, if you will — which would have had a difficult time adjusting to each other under the most favourable of conditions — and conditions were far from favourable during the entire entanglement.

On the one hand, Graham delights in taking responsibility for his actions and is deeply concerned with operating his business at maximum efficiency. He clearly regards the Fillmore East as "my property, since I pay the rent." On the other hand, the amorphous "community", a coalition of various factions without any duly appointed leadership, seems to reject any collective responsibility, preferring instead the protection of segmental camouflage.

The dispute goes to the heart of capitalism: who owns what. Graham is into "property"; Ben Morea, Motherfuckers' spokesman, feels that "property is the least consideration. The most important thing is people's lives and living. One of the basic things in *our* culture is the absence of property, or the lack of respect for property."

Morea continues: "The Fillmore's interests are not our interests, and that's the conflict. They're a business. We are not a business — we're a people who feel we have a culture which we want access to, that's been taken from us, and that's being used to make money for other people. We don't want just a show, we want to go back to those original attempts at having a community culture, not a money-making thing. By nature of the conflict, they're into making money, and we're into living. They're somewhere else, which we don't dig and which is bullshit."

Here is what Kip Cohen, manager of Fillmore East, thinks of the Motherfuckers: "Oddly enough, the Motherfuckers, as an organisation, while they may not be the most passive of the community factions, have become the spokesmen for the community — and the community has allowed them to become the spokesmen. When all the trouble was occurring, we were extremely disappointed in some of the saner members of the community who allowed this to go on without speaking up, the basic point being that it seemed that no one was willing to lose his cool by standing up and making a statement."

It is plain to see why the twain never *really* met.

Play *Rashomon* with us now as we examine various viewpoints about several key incidents.

The WBAI-FM caper

Cohen claims that, in late October, the Motherfuckers, as representatives of the community, made their initial demands to "liberate" the Fillmore East for one free night a week over radio station WBAI-FM. According to Bob Rudnick and Dennis Frawley, rock columnists for *The East Village Other*, the community planned to use the hall for "free food, music, dancing, smoke, tumbling, nude dancing, and a flock of meetings ... a free exchange of goods and energy."

Graham was eventually approached on the matter, but only after subsequent demands were made in the form of pamphlets distributed in the East Village. He said that he would have to approve the community's plans first. According to Cohen, their answer was: "Man, we ain't got time. Next Wednesday is our first show." Graham lost his temper and ordered them out of the building.

Morea denies a good deal of this. He claims that Graham, in *early* October, agreed to let the community use the hall one night a week, but later changed his mind "for no reason. *None* of the Motherfuckers were *ever* on WBAI, there's no question about that. But there *were* other groups involved."

Ah, semantics.

The Living Theater Benefit

Both sides are in basic agreement on what happened in the early part of the evening. Morea: "We spoke to the Living Theater. They agreed that we should have the free night. So on the night of their benefit for Columbia University strikers [held at the Fillmore], we decided to appeal to the audience to try and make it clear to Graham that a lot of people felt that the demand for one night a week was not out of the question.

"That night the Living Theater did *Paradise Now*, but the performance was interrupted when somebody announced from the stage that the people were here and uptight about not having the theater. Graham came on stage and went through his whole riff with us about how 'You'll never get this theater' and all that shit. So nobody left the theater for a couple of hours. We negotiated with Graham, and he agreed to give us a night in the next week for a town meeting."

According to Cohen, the argument raged well into the early hours of the morning and the "town meeting" was to be at least partially a debate between Graham and the community.

Morea: "No, it was *not* to be a debate. They gave it to us as a community assembly night to discuss what we would do with the Fillmore. They weren't supposed to debate with us whether we'd get it or not."

The Town Meeting or the Debate

Cohen claims that, on arrival, the Motherfuckers told Graham (who had flown in from San Francisco especially for the meeting): "Fuck you. Fuck your goddamn town meetings. We don't need to talk. We don't need to rap. This is a fuck-in, man. We're here to have a good time. This is our crash pad for the winter. Can you dig it?" At midnight, they finally agreed to talk. An angry Graham told them that he did not recognize the Motherfuckers as true representatives of the community and once again ordered them out of the hall. Retaliations were threatened and the "debate" ended with "minor skirmishes and minor damage to property. Once again, we had to wait it out until they all left."

Morea: "When we got there, Graham had the stage set up with two tables and a lot of microphones. He told us that it was a debate between us and him. We said that we weren't there to debate, we were there to talk to *ourselves*, to eat together, to hear some music together, and to have a community night — and *not* to debate him. But he wasn't excluded."

The Free Nights and the Law

Cohen:"After the debate, some responsible members of the community asked to see us and told us they didn't dig what went down that night either. They asked permission to come to us with a proper and responsible program. Our answer was an obvious yes. They came back a couple of days later with creative, constructive measures, and we agreed to give them free use of the Fillmore East each Wednesday night.

"The first free night, in late November, was organized with music and workshops, but the theater was full of Bowery bums, winos, people just dropping by, and speed freaks from St. Mark's Place, who were not about to partake in anything creative. It was plain there would be obvious problems with the law." (Graham later specified them in an "open letter" to the community as "smoking on the premises, incidents of physical confrontation, and the blatant use, distribution and sale of drugs on the premises — obviously illegal."

Morea agrees that "There was one problem — dope. There was free use of dope, or fairly free. The police became very uptight because they knew they couldn't come in there and stop it because there were, like, a thousand people *acting freely*. So they pressured Graham and told him they were going to close his theater down unless it was stopped. We told Graham that we would try to stop it in the way we could. We could never stop people from using dope altogether — that's not part of our thing — but we could try and get them to cool it in the Fillmore. The next week, we made some announcements about it from the stage in, to be honest, a not-too-heavy manner. Some of it did stop, but there was still some use of it."

Cohen: "Inspector Pine from the First Division came down and asked us what had been going on on free nights. We told him, and then *he* told *us* — and knew the story in greater detail than we did. He asked us what we could do to control it. I said I didn't think we could do anything to control it since the green shirt of a Fillmore East usher wasn't about to be respected by the Motherfuckers. He told us that unless a conscious attempt was made to control certain problems, we would be in jeopardy of losing our license to operate. We told the community, and they said they understood.

"The following free night was a little better. The Wednesday after that was very bad. There was open dope smoking and damage to property. All through the free nights, sound equipment was constantly stolen or damaged — hundreds of dollars' worth every single week."

Morea denies that equipment was stolen from and damage done to the hall: "There might have been, like, one seat or something wrecked, but there was *no essential damage* on any of these nights."

Graham's "Open Letter"

Again the law — this time with a *final* warning. Graham circulated his "open letter" to the community via a public relations firm and pamphlets declaring the end of the free nights. He urged everyone "to *accept our predicament* (which is now *your* reality) with intelligence, understanding and grace."

The Motherfuckers circulated an answer: "Situation: Pigs and Bill Graham stop free night. Why? They say we smoke, they say we take dope, but we know it's because they are afraid of us. Afraid that we'll learn it's ours. Afraid that we'll get together there to destroy their world and create our own.

"The pigs threaten to close Graham down unless he stops our free night. He doesn't have to worry about the pigs. We'll close him down. No free night, no pay night. Thursday night they scheduled a 'free' concert for Elektra Records. We'll be there. And Friday and Saturday and always. The Lower East Side community has lost the use of the Fillmore. The Fillmore must lose the use of the community."

On the Monday before Christmas, which was to have been a free night because of the Wednesday holiday, the doors of the Fillmore East were locked and the police told to stay away. According to Morea, the Motherfuckers had asked to use the hall that night "not as a free night, but to discuss the use and non-use of dope in connection with the whole problem." The request was refused. Morea: "Kip Cohen, who was somewhat sympathetic, called Graham in California. Graham said, 'I don't owe these people anything.'"

The MC5 Concert

Thursday, December 26. All hell broke loose. Elektra had rented the hall to present the MC5 and had given 2300 tickets to local radio stations to give away

"A strange thing happened. The minute that they saw the blood on Bill's face, there was a strong reaction from the crowd, and these hundreds of people who had been swarming on top of him backed away. A lot of people were very disgusted, and it seemed to be a turning point in the whole thing."

Morea: "Graham knows, more or less, all of us. I'm sure he could tell you that it was *not* one of us who struck him."

The evening went on, and the concert ended. Most people left. However, about four hundred to five hundred people stayed and according to Cohen, "swarmed on the stage and started their big jumping, screaming, freaking kind of thing. As you looked up at the stage, you wondered if this was the total creative effort that the East Village community could come up with: Bowery bums and young ten- and eleven-year-old kids with sticks bounding around the stage.

"They were banging on the MC5's equipment and broke a drumhead. The MC5 split in a Limousine rented by Elektra to Max's Kansas City for dinner, a not-too-unusual move for a rock group under any circumstances. It was not received too well. A Motherfucker at the mike made a public announcement about what the group was doing, a crowd swarmed outside, pulled them out of their car, messed them up a bit, threw their records at them, came back in, and announced to the crowd that they had been betrayed by phonies'.

"That seemed to be the end of the MC5 with this particular audience of four hundred people. It was ironic and somewhat strangely amusing."

Did Morea feel that the MC5 had betrayed the community? "Oh, yeah, absolutely. They projected themselves as a 'revolutionary' rock group. They knew that there was something going on that was much deeper than politics, that had to do with exactly what they talk about: cultural revolution. They knew they could play a certain role. Nobody asked *them* to seize the theater, but there was no question that they could have done *something*. In fact, they did the opposite. They stood up there and said 'We're here to play music and we don't give a damn about politics.'

"Then, they ran out, symbolically getting into a limousine going to a restaurant which *nobody* in our community has *ever* been in. The whole image of that was rather obnoxious."

The evening droned on. Graham had made an agreement to go to the police to see if anything could be done about another free night for the community.

Cohen: "*After* the agreement was made, someone was hit over the head with a microphone and hospitalized, a young Puerto Rican boy was stabbed, and one of our ushers had his arm fractured with a metal pipe. In addition to that, one thousand dollars' worth of equipment was damaged or stolen and the asbestos stage curtain slashed by knives."

Did the Motherfuckers feel in any way responsible for the injuries and the damage? Not for a moment! Morea: "Well, nobody could take responsibility *except* Graham. Because Graha.n, as far as everybody is concerned, caused it all by taking away the free nights and thus creating the tension. In fact, we have a letter from Graham which states that we are *not* responsible for the damage. He knows that it was the result of a misunderstanding.

"We are all sorry that certain things happened. I'm not particularly sorry about Graham's theater — because I don't care too much about his theater — but I *do* care about people being assaulted."

Graham, using the words "filthy, low-life scum," *did* later place the blame for the damage on the Motherfuckers and on a motorcycle gang called the Pagans who he claims were "brought in to 'liberate' the Fillmore."

The Aftermath

The next day, Graham felt he could no longer support the community even to the extent of going down to the police station as he said he would. Cohen: "We've been raped publicly six times by now, and it's a question of how many times you can take it. That Friday, a lot of people from the community began to see that maybe we weren't such bad guys after all."

Morea's only comment on the "rape" statement was "Well, that might have something to do with his own psychological thing."

On the evening of December 27, WBAI presented a forum on the Fillmore East-Motherfucker problem. As a result of this broadcast, Graham's insurance company threatened to terminate the hall's fire and liability cover completely. The Motherfuckers were informed. According to Cohen, their reaction was: "'Fuck insurance. Fuck the insurance man. We don't care.'"

The choice

Cohen: "On Saturday, December 28, the important thing happened. Bill said to the community: "Look, when are you going to face up to the fact that you've blown it here? You can't have the Fillmore. You have made that impossible.' Their answer was: '*You* made it this way. *You* resisted us. *You* caused the trouble.'

"Then Bill said: 'Look, I'm not trying to buy you off, but *you* find another place, *you* find a constructive, realistic program that works within the framework of the law — even if it is inherently an attempt to change that law — and *I* will support it. I'll support it administratively, I'll support it technically, I'll see that you get talent over there, and I'll support it financially.'

"And he laid it out — very, very detailed. Some of them said, 'Yes, this makes sense. Let's do it.' Some of the Motherfuckers said, 'No, we want the Fillmore.' Bill described figures of several thousand dollars a month."

The community is still meeting and mulling to come up with an answer to the proposal. According to Morea, "We can either find another insurance company —

which Graham can pay for — and continue to have the free nights at the Fillmore, or we can take his money to pay the rent on an alternate spot. We're discussing both possibilities now. The majority feel they want the money to have their own place, but some people feel that we should have the Fillmore because it's part of our culture — and we want access to it for that reason.

"If no insurance company will cover the Fillmore, we can understand that. It's obvious that you can't force somebody to do something they can't do. That's why there has been no pressure on Graham or the hall in the past few weeks."

January

For the moment everyone is playing the waiting game. All is quiet on the Eastern Front. Ironically, throughout all of the turmoil, the most eloquent defences of the other side's point of view came from the adversaries themselves.

Said Cohen of the Motherfuckers and the community: "A lot of these people were in Chicago during the Democratic Convention. If some of them say, 'This is what I think about a cop,' a lot of them have a very good reason to make that statement."

Answered Morea, not one to be outdone at anything: "I don't feel that the Fillmore *ever* distorted the facts."

Peace.

— February 15, 1969

SECTION SEVEN

BEN MOREA

INTERVIEW

Ben Morea was interviewed by Iain McIntyre in 2006. This interview as published first appeared in *Up Against the Wall Motherfucker!*, Homebrew Press, 2007. An edited version of this interview along with commentary from Dan Georgakas appeared in *Realizing the Impossible: Art Against Authority*, AK Press, 2007.

Tell us about your background and how you came to find yourself involved in the radical scenes of New York during the 1960s.

I was raised mostly around the Virginia/Maryland area and New York. When I was ten years old my mother remarried and moved to Manhattan. I was basically a ghetto kid and got involved in drug addictions as a teenager spending time in prison. At one point when I was in a prison hospital I started reading and developed an interest in art. When I was released I completely changed my persona. In order to break my addiction I made a complete break from the kids I grew up with and the life I knew.

In the late 1950s I went looking for the beatniks because they seemed to combine social awareness with art. I met the Living Theatre people and was highly influenced by their ideas despite never being theatrically oriented myself. Judith Malina and Julian Beck were anarchists and they were the first people to put a name to the way I was feeling and leaning philosophically.

I also met an Italian-American artist named Aldo Tambellini who was very radical in his thinking and who channelled all of that into his art rather than social activism. He would only hold shows in common areas like churchyards and hallways in order to bring art to the public. He influenced me a lot in seeing that having art in museums was a way of rarefying it and making it a tool of the ruling class.

I'm self educated and continued my pursuit of anarchism and art through reading and correspondence. I became aware of Dada and Surrealism and the radical wing of twentieth century art and sought out anyone who had information about it or who had been involved. I really felt comfortable with the wedding of social thought with aesthetic practice. I corresponded quite a bit with one of the living Dadaists Richard Huelsenbeck who was living in New York, but whom I never met.

At the same time I became friendly with the political wing of the anarchists meeting up with people who had fought in Spain, from the Durutti Brigade and other groups. They were all in their 60s and I was in my 20s.

I was also a practising artist working at my own art and aesthetic. I was mainly painting in an abstract, but naturalistic form as well as doing some sculpture. There was some influence from the American expressionists, but Zen was also an influence.

When did Black Mask come together as a group? How were you organised and who was involved?

It's hard to say whether we started in 1965 or 1966, but the magazine definitely started in 1966. Black Mask was really very small. It started off with just a few people. As anarchists, and not very doctrinaire ones, we had no leadership although I was the driving force in the group. Both Ron Hahne and I had already been working together with Aldo doing art shows in public to promote the idea of art as an integral part of everyday life, not an institutionalised thing.

Ron and I became close friends and found that we had a more socially polemical view than Aldo in wanting to go closer to the political elements of Dada and Surrealism as well as to the growing unrest in Black America. We wanted to find a place where art and politics could coexist in a radical way. Once we started publishing *Black Mask* and holding actions other artists and people on a similar wavelength were attracted to what we were doing. I've always favoured an organic approach where you don't have meetings and people just associate informally rather than having a hierarchy and recruiting members.

Over time Ron became less interested in the political sphere and I became more interested in working with the people who were involved in fighting for civil rights and against the Vietnam war.

I can honestly say that in both Black Mask and then later The Family we never held a meeting where we consciously sat down to decide our direction or exactly how we would deal with a particular action or situation. It all developed as a very spontaneous, organic outgrowth of whatever we thought was appropriate at the time.

One of Black Mask's first actions was to shut down the Museum Of Modern Art (MOMA). Tell us about what happened and the group's approach to direct action in general.

We felt that art itself, the creative effort, was an obviously worthwhile, valuable and even spiritual experience. The Museum and gallery system separated art from that living interchange and had nothing to do with the vital, creative urge. Museums weren't a living house, they were just a repository. We were searching for ways to raise questions about how things were presented and closing down MOMA was just one of them.

The action was a success. We'd announced our plans in advance and they closed the museum in fear of what we might do. A lot of people stopped and talked with us about what we were doing and this action and others attracted radical artists to our fold.

At other times we disrupted exhibitions, galleries and lectures. Most of these actions were just thought up on the spot and a lot of what we did was part of a learning process. Things weren't completely thought out, but were a way for us to develop an understanding of our place in the ongoing struggle. A lot of political groups would have these big grandiose strategies and plans, but for us the actions were just a way of expressing ourselves and seeing how we could make a dent in society.

In 1966 the group also targeted the Loeb Center at New York University (NYU). What happened with that action?

We had a strong sense of humour and of guerrilla theatre. I used to disrupt art lectures at NYU to raise issues other than those that the lecturers wanted to discuss. As a result I was challenged to a debate by some of the academics. I remember that particular event had such a pretentious approach that we had to do something. It was incredibly stratified and only meant for the elite and it seemed like they'd done everything possible to keep it away from the public at large. We handed out loads of leaflets advertising this free event with food and alcohol and they had to block off the streets all around because so many people showed up. We went down to the Bowery and handed out flyers so that all the drunks and street people would show up.

Black Mask clearly drew inspiration not only from the Dadaists, Surrealists and avant-garde movements of the past, but also from the contemporary black insurrections and youth movements of the 1960s. Tell us a little more about these influences and about your ideas and approach to politics and art in general.

From my perspective and that of the people I worked with we saw a need to change everything from the way we lived to the way we thought to the way we even ate. Total Revolution was our way of saying that we weren't going to settle for political or cultural change, but that we want it all, we want everything to change. Western society had reached a stalemate and needed a total overhaul. We knew that wasn't going to happen, but that was our demand, what we were about.

It also meant seeing that you need all types of people involved, not just political activists. Poets and artists are just as important. Revolution comes about as a cumulative effect and part of that is a change in consciousness, a new way of thinking.

How did Black Mask fit into the New York political and arts scenes because it seems as if you went out of your way to ridicule and challenge ideologues of all stripes?

A lot of political people questioned what we did saying we should only attack society on the political front and that we shouldn't care about art. However we felt it was best to take action in the place where you were and that as artists these issues were important to us.

Many of the hippies distrusted us and the politicos hated us because they couldn't control us or understand what we were doing. As for the people in the art world I'm sure most of them thought we were crazy.

Black Mask seems to have issued various challenges to the peace movement in criticising the moderates for their lack of militancy whilst also attacking the Left for its unconditional support of the National Liberation Front (NLF). Many radicals from the 1960s are now somewhat regretful or appear reticent to speak about their support for the North Vietnamese regime.

We supported the right of the Vietnamese people to resist American invasion, but were not going to support the North Vietnamese government's own oppressive behaviour. It was a subtle point and most of the left couldn't understand it. We knew the history of Spain where both the Francoists and Stalinists executed anarchists. We refused to support one side or the other.

I hated the knee jerk reaction of much of the Left who delighted in waving the NLF flag around. We didn't cheer the killing of American troops who were stuck over there as cannon fodder like some others did.

In a sense we didn't fit in anywhere and that meant we became a pole of attraction for all those other people who weren't interested in a dogmatic or pacifistic approach. Much of the later evolution of Black Mask into The Family came about through more and more of these people joining with us and affecting where we were going.

Black Mask and later The Family were some of the first groups to encourage the concept of affinity groups as a way of organising. One Family member famously defined an affinity group as a "street gang with analysis." How did this approach develop and the use of term come about?

Although we associated in similar circles with Murray Bookchin our group was always very different because we were very visceral and he was very literate. Murray was keen on using the Spanish term aficionado de vairos to describe these non-hierarchical groupings of people that were happening. We said "Oh my god, can you really imagine Americans calling themselves aficionado de vairos?" (laughter) "Use English, call them affinity groups."

Tell us about the Black Mask *magazine you produced which ran from 1966 to 1968 and spanned ten issues.*

Ron and I mainly put the magazine together, but there was a wider group who helped produce, print and distribute it. We sold it for a nickel, which wasn't much money, but we figured if people had to pay for it then they would actually want and read it rather than just take one look and throw it in the trash.

We tended to sell it on the Lower East Side, which was the most fertile ground for us as there were many artists and activists. We occasionally went up town as well although that was more to stir the pot.

Black Mask was one of the first groups to take on countercultural figures like Timothy Leary and Allen Ginsberg for their timidity, orientation towards religion and status seeking, labelling them at one point "The New Establishment." From 1967 onwards it seems as if Black Mask moved a lot of its critique away from the arts establishment and towards the growing hippy movement and New Left.

Although we were critical of them I was close to Allen Ginsberg and became close to Timothy Leary years later. What we were trying to say at that moment was that they were allowing themselves to be used as a safety valve. We wanted to attack the core of society and believed they weren't doing that. At the time we thought they were being used by the likes of *Time* and *Life Magazine* although in hindsight *Time* and *Life* probably wish they had never covered them, especially Timothy.

We were always trying to shake things up, to push everyone else as well as ourselves. There was always a lot of interchange with all sorts of other radicals and sometimes there was fratricide in that we would strike out at people we otherwise liked just to make a point.

In 1966 Black Mask *magazine cited the Situationist International as a group moving in a similar direction to yourselves calling as they were for "the revolution of everyday life" and the abolition of art as a separate, specialized activity. However in late 1967 the SI expelled three of its British members for having supported "a certain Ben Morea, publisher of the bulletin* Black Mask.*" What was the source of friction between the groups and to what extent were you ever linked?*

The Situationists and I never saw eye to eye. I thought that they were extremely doctrinaire and limited. The Situationists seemed to excommunicate more people than they kept. There was never really any connection between our groups and theirs.

What happened with the "assassination" of the poet Ken Koch in 1967?

Koch was a symbol to us of this totally bourgeois, dandy world. Myself, Dan Georgakas, Alan Van Newkirk and some of the other Black Mask people went to one of his readings. I think I came up with idea to shoot him with a blank pistol. Alan looked like the classic image of the bomb throwing anarchist. He was about six foot three, long and thin with a gaunt face and always dressed in black- the anarchist incarnate. So we decided "You're the one, you're going to shoot him." (laughter) We printed a leaflet and all it had on it was a picture of Leroi Jones with the words 'Poetry is revolution.' On the night when Alan shot the blank Koch fainted and everyone in the audience assumed he was dead and started screaming. Some people threw the leaflet from the balcony into the crowd and then we all left.

Reactions after the event were split between people who thought it was the greatest thing they'd ever heard and those that thought we were a bunch of sophomoric assholes. Which was great because so much of what Black Mask and The Family was about was pushing people to decide "Do I belong with this group of people or this one?" We were determined to be outrageous in order to force people to decide where they stood on things. We wanted to push people, force them to think. "Why shoot Koch? He's just a nice poet."

What was Black Mask's connection to Students for a Democratic Society?

We saw that SDS was becoming a real force for change and that all these traditional left groups and Maoists like Progressive Labor were trying to take it over and control its direction. We thought it was important for other kinds of people, like us, to get involved and show the students that there were many choices, many ways they could go.

I remember being at one of the SDS national conventions and people were getting into a heated debate about the differences between the Yankees, the East Coast based establishment, and the Cowboys, the Texan based establishment. I got up and said "This is all bullshit, I don't know about you guys, we're not the Yankees or the Cowboys- we're the Indians!" Another time a member of The Family ran for a position and got up with a waste paper basket and said "Here's my platform, throw all the position papers in here."

With both Black Mask and later The Family we used guerrilla theatre and actions to show that there was another approach on offer other than boring politics as usual and the more volatile elements of SDS resonated with that. Some of the people who went on to form [US armed struggle organisation] The Weathermen hung out with The Family and, although it has never really been credited, borrowed a lot from our militant style and attitude. However once they melded with the more Leninist groups they took it all in a very different direction.

Tell us about Valerie Solanas, who you were close to and wrote a defence of following her murder attempt on Andy Warhol in 1968. There was a deafening silence in the underground press around her ideas and actions following the shooting. This seems a little odd given the fact that by this point the New Left had begun to increasingly glorify political violence.

Valerie used to stay with me quite a bit as she was fairly homeless and always on the move. There was a lot of parody and irony in her writing, but she was also, and I don't mean this in a bad sense, a fairly crazy person. She saw a need to raise a lot of issues around what happens to women and the *SCUM Manifesto* was the best way she could express herself. I always loved people who were loose cannons, who didn't fit the mould.

Sometime later when Black Mask had wrapped up and The Family had started we were involved in the occupation of Columbia University [1968]. Valerie came up there and found me and asked "What would happen if I shot somebody?" I said "It depends on two things- who you shoot and whether they die or not." A week later she shot Andy Warhol.

After she shot him I wrote a pamphlet supporting her. I may have been the only person who did that publicly. I went up to MOMA and handed it out there. Everybody I met was very negative about it, but, hey, I disliked Andy Warhol immensely and I loved Valerie. I felt she was right in her anger and that he was way more destructive than she was because he was helping to destroy the whole idea of creativity in art. Some people dislike the term, but I feel that creativity is a kind of spiritual act, a profound thing for people to do. Warhol was the exact opposite, he tried to deny and purge the core of creativity and put it on a commercial basis. As a person he was really despicable, as well, and that's why Valerie hated him. He used and manipulated people.

The attack on Andy was met with silence on the Left and I think that was because it raised issues that no one could deal with. This wasn't violence occurring in some far off place. Also Andy had become a star, almost an honoured image, and here she was striking at it. Even the people who liked her feminist approach couldn't deal with the fact that she would harm Andy. Black Mask and The Family drove the political people nuts because we didn't fit into any of their blueprints, because we were loose cannons, so you can imagine how they looked upon Valerie.

Black Mask continued *as a magazine until mid-1968. What was the process by which the group began to evolve and change into what became known as* Up Against the Wall Motherfucker?

The Family/Up Against The Wall Motherfucker and Black Mask were related in that one grew into the other, but in reality they were very separate groups in terms of the people involved and what they did. There was no decision to start a new group, no blueprint, it was just an evolutionary thing where one died away and the next thing came to be. It's hard even to say exactly at which point one ended and the next began.

The Family went over the edge, was extremely volatile and didn't have as much inclination toward the cultural sphere. It included a lot of artists, but also people from all persuasions who wanted to live a life more real, more visceral than what was offered. Something less limiting than just pursuing politics or art, something freer.

We weren't really hippies or politicos. We were separate from other groups even though we were part of the wider counterculture. Some people would have placed us as hippies. Those that knew something about the counterculture could sense that we were a much more guttural breed. But outwardly we did have the trappings of the hippies in terms of long hair and ethnic clothing. We also took a lot of LSD. Even though we were also radicals no one would have mixed us up with the Young Communist League. (laughter)

What were some of the differences between Black Mask and The Family?

The Family was much bigger and more vital than Black Mask which was more of an esoteric group. We never called ourselves Up Against The

Wall Motherfucker, although we signed our posters and leaflets UAW/ MF, which anyone in the group could produce, with that name. Amongst ourselves we were The Family, which might sound weird now because of the association of that name with Charles Manson with whom we had no connection and nothing in common with.

Whereas I was the main figure in Black Mask, The Family was quite different because it involved a large group of people who were all equal in strength and in determining the direction of the group. It was essentially a loose confederation of affinity groups living across a series of crash pads who shared a tribal outlook and lifestyle. Different people from the core group would gravitate to a particular address where a lot of young hippies and runaways would also stay.

The fact that we rejected the nuclear family model and lived collectively was never arrived at in a polemical fashion or laid out as a blueprint. We just had a sense that there were other roots to living other than what the West had to offer, whether it was from Native Americans, gypsies or Africa. The hippies had some of that too, but we really leaned heavily towards this tribal, ethnic outlook. We felt that there was some strength there that transcended the Western world. We tried to understand and incorporate some of these elements, both in our appearance and actual living style. Our whole lives were directed towards free flow, living organically.

Tell us about the actions The Family were involved in.

The first real action we did as The Family was to take garbage to the Lincoln Centre in February 1968. There was a garbage strike in New York and there was tons of refuse mounting up in the ghettos. The commercial and wealthier areas were able to hire private contractors to clean their streets so we decided to take some of the garbage from the Lower East Side up to the Lincoln Centre. One of our members proposed this as a cultural exchange- garbage for garbage (laughter). Although others tended to focus on our aggression and militancy we really had some beautifully witty people.

We put out a leaflet explaining why we were doing this, but those of us involved realised that we weren't really Black Mask anymore and so we didn't want that name on it. There was a poem by Leroi Jones with the line "Up Against The Wall Mother Fucker" in it and I suggested we put that on there. Somehow it stuck and from then on in everyone referred to us as that. It wasn't a deliberate thing on our part. It would have been fairly pretentious to just name ourselves "The Motherfuckers." (laughter) *Black Mask* continued as a magazine for a little longer and then UAW/MF started creating flyers and posters and doing things for papers like *The Rat.*

How were those broadsheets and statements put together?
They were part of our artistic politics and we enjoyed putting them together either individually or as a group. We wanted to do something that was creative and visually exciting, but which also made a statement. With *The Rat* two to six members of The Family would go up to their office each week and do our page. Whoever felt inspired would come along and we'd all collaborate. People who have reprinted our work, both at the time and since, often failed to appreciate our sense of humour. We believed in what we were doing, but we didn't want to be too serious. We could laugh at ourselves. The best influence we felt we could have was not just to inject militancy, but also joy and humour into the struggles of the time.

We had our own mimeograph machine so people were constantly running off leaflets and posters. A lot of the time I would see one on the street that I didn't even know had come out. The beauty of our family was that it was multi-armed and had no central brain so people were often doing actions and producing things that the rest knew little about.

In the group's writings an affinity group was defined as a "street gang with analysis." How much of the traditional street gang mentality was a part of your outlook though?
Some members were more into the street thing than others. We weren't territorial or into dead end opposition however. We were "street tough" rather than street toughs. Osha Neumann who penned that particular definition (though I had coined the term Affinity Group) saw it as meaning that we had street smarts and an intense bond not that we were irrational bullies.

In 1968 students struck and occupied buildings at Columbia in a protest against the redevelopment of land earmarked for social housing and the university's links to weapons research. How were you guys involved?
There were five buildings occupied at Columbia and the one we were in was the only one the police didn't attack. We didn't put a call out, but everyone who was a fighter gravitated towards that building. We were so fortified and aggressive that having evicted all the others they decided to negotiate rather than force their way in.

We didn't operate from any plan, we just saw situations and took our chances. We were edge dwellers. During the anti-war protests at the

Pentagon we saw the doors weren't heavily guarded so we went for it and broke them open. We'd gone along with all the other protesters, but pretty soon we attracted a core of a few hundred people who were like us. We saw an opportunity, made a move and they came along.

During 1968 and 1969 The Family were also involved in resisting police harassment and violence on the Lower East Side. How did you go about dealing with these problems?

Our response would include everything from peaceful protests to not peaceful battling depending on the situation. We were extremely volatile and it often depended on how hard we were pushed.

Eventually they decided that we had to be dealt with. One night we barricaded the streets to traffic and threw a party. The police came, but saw we had too many people and were too strong so they left us alone. However that was the beginning of the end. We'd become too cocky and uncontrollable and they began busting us for anything they could.

In October 1968 you personally faced trial on charges of attempted murder in Boston. What led up to this and your eventual acquittal?

While I was in New York we heard that young freaks, we never called ourselves hippies, were being harassed by this group of vigilantes in Boston. It was pretty bad and a few kids had been hospitalised so I suggested to some Family members that we should go there and look into it. We went up and stayed with the street kids and freaks and sure enough they were attacked while we were there. The attackers were repelled and I was charged by the police.

I was in jail for about two weeks before I raised bail. After I stood trial we heard that these vigilantes were still hurting people and decided to go back because we were concerned that we may have made things worse. The same guys turned up again, but this time they backed down and disappeared which was lucky for me because it wouldn't have done my cause any good.

I didn't get a lot of support for my case as the political community couldn't have cared less about the hippies whilst the hippies were for the most part non-violent. However various people helped out and the story got some coverage in the underground press. In the end I was acquitted, but the foreman told me that it was all down to one juror. On the first vote it was 11 to 1 in favour of convicting me, but one guy managed to convince the others that there was enough doubt to let me go. I don't know who he was, but I owe that one guy my liberty.

Other than supporting people against the police and opening crash pads The Family also ran a free store and was involved in various other activities aimed at street level survival. Tell us about these activities.

We were always trying to connect the hippy part of the Lower East Side community with the street and homeless part. With the influx of thousands of runaways into the area during the late 1960s they were sometimes one and the same, but the two communities didn't always comfortably coexist. We set up a store front to give homeless people as well as ourselves a place to hang out. We had free clothes, doctors and lawyers on retainers, a mimeograph, information for people who wanted to dodge the draft and get fake ID, information on crash pads, etc. It was a general help centre. We did free food a couple of nights a week, but also held free food events in a hall or a church on the others where we would feed up to 300-400 people. We got some papers from a church saying we were a non-profit and that allowed us to get day old or incorrectly marked stuff from the produce markets and food outlets for free. Some people worked, others made donations and the same papers also helped us to hustle up grants from liberal churches to rent places, etc.

As with a lot of other countercultural groups at the time The Family drew a line between 'life drugs' and 'death drugs.' Tell us about that and the group's approach to illicit drugs in general.

We differentiated between hard drugs like cocaine and heroin and those like grass, hashish and psychedelics. We saw that LSD and grass were helping to break down the structures between suburban youth and helping them to rethink their place in the universe. Some of us had had problems with hard drugs and saw that they were destructive. Unlike Leary and others we didn't see psychedelics as a cure all, but they could and did make a positive contribution.

People would sometimes bring kids to me who were on bad trips. I would take LSD and try to go with them to the place where they were in trouble and help them come back. If you want to talk about putting yourself out there, that was it. You wouldn't see many Maoists doing that. (laughter)

In late 1968 The Family went head to head with rock promoter Bill Graham over the issue of community involvement in the Fillmore East venue. What were the origins of the dispute and how did it all pan out?

At root this was a clash between the grassroots and those who exploit them. We didn't want control of the Fillmore East or anything

like that, but we wanted to have one free, non commercial night for the
street people. Given the money they were making out of the community
we figured that they could give something back.

At first Graham refused and during one meeting in his office he
pulled out three silver bullets and lined them up saying "The Hells Angels
made similar demands on me and sent me these three bullets and I didn't
give in." I got up and said "There's one difference between us and the
Angels, we're not giving you anything to put on your desk." That wasn't
a literal threat, but a statement that one way or another we were going
to get what we were demanding.

One night the Living Theatre people were performing at the Fillmore
East and we arranged to come up on stage after them. I made a statement
saying that they were finished, but we were going to stay on stage for as
long as it would take to get what we wanted. It might take one night, two
nights or two weeks, but we were going to stay. We occupied the stage
and fights broke out through the night with Graham and his goons, but
they lost and at about one or two in the morning he gave in and we got
the Thursday night for free.

What sort of events happened on the free Thursdays?

A lot of rock bands including Canned Heat, the MC5 and Country
Joe McDonald came and played for free and we gave out free dope and
food. I've been told that the MC5 clashed with some sections of the
crowd, but I remember staying at their place in Michigan some time later
so I'm not sure what happened there. After three weeks Graham came
to me with a letter from the police informing him that they were going
to shut the whole venue down if these nights continued due to the free
drugs policy. We accepted that that was it, but in the end it didn't matter
that it had only lasted three weeks because we got to challenge the whole
commercial world of rock n' roll.

Woodstock provided us with another opportunity to challenge the
music industry. These young kids said "You always say the music's free,
well we're going to make it free." Like most of the things we did nothing
was planned. We just went along and some of us thought it would be a
good idea to cut the fences and let everyone in. When it began raining
we found where the organisers were storing camping equipment for sale
and liberated all the tents and sleeping bags. We cut a hole in the storage
tent and just gave them out.

Did The Family interact much with groups from other parts of the country and world?

A tremendous number of people came through New York and spent time with us around the time that The Family began. They included some UK Situationists who became the King Mob group, members of the Zenga-Kuren from Japan, Jean Jacques Leibel who was one of the leaders in the '68 uprising in Paris and also some Provos from Holland. All of these groups overlapped with our approach in one way or another.

We were also doing a lot of travelling ourselves. I spent time with The Diggers in San Francisco. They were coming from a very similar place in terms of radicalism and the rejection of the entrepreneurs who were profiting from the counterculture, but our approaches were very different. There was a lot of support from the West Coast groups, even [LSD manufacturer] Owsley gave us some money. There were also small groups of people all over the country who identified with us and stayed with us

What prompted the decision to leave the Lower East Side?

The police felt threatened by us. They began following us closely and engaging in constant harassment. Some of our people were also charged in the second wave of indictments that came out of the Chicago protests.

These things in themselves didn't drive us out, but we were evolving and exploring new directions. The tribal element became more strident and many of us began to wonder why we were stuck in the ghetto anyway. A lot of the young runaways were being preyed upon and we felt it would be safer to move them out . We took about twenty of them to California at one point and helped others find homes elsewhere.

The group didn't end all of a sudden, but dispersed with most of us getting involved in various land oriented projects and communes. I personally stopped writing and went into the mountains and didn't come out for five years. I became inspired by Wilhelm Reich's *The Murder of Christ* and its idea that you don't ignore the wider issues, but move on to tackle them one person at a time.

With the US government on a permanent war footing overseas whilst simultaneously cracking down on civil liberties and dissent at home it sometimes seems as if the left wing movements of the 1960s never existed. What do you see as the legacy of groups like Black Mask and the New Left in general?

Part of the reason I re-emerged [after more than 30 years of anonymity] to talk about what we did back in the 1960s is the fact that things have gotten so bad in the US. It's at a point where you can't ignore it, it's worse than ever.

I figured that I'd start letting people know about our history and then go from there. All I can tell people is that when it looked pretty dismal in the past we took action and it did have an effect. A lot was achieved and yet a few years beforehand no one would have expected that we could take on the behemoth of American capitalism. It's counter-productive to sit back and say "You can't do anything." It's not my place to tell people exactly what they should do, but there is always some way to respond and take action, just look around.

Other than giving occasional talks Ben has returned to painting and also contributes his opinions to a regular blog which can be found at http://e-blast.squarespace.com

The Angry Brigade: A History of Britain's First Urban Guerilla Group
Gordon Carr

978-1-60486-049-8
$24.95

"You can't reform profit capitalism and inhumanity. Just kick it till it breaks."
— Angry Brigade, communiqué.

Between 1970 and 1972, the Angry Brigade used guns and bombs in a series of symbolic attacks against property. A series of communiqués accompanied the actions, explaining the choice of targets and the Angry Brigade philosophy: autonomous organization and attacks on property alongside other forms of militant working class action. Targets included the embassies of repressive regimes, police stations and army barracks, boutiques and factories, government departments and the homes of Cabinet ministers, the Attorney General and the Commissioner of the Metropolitan Police. These attacks on the homes of senior political figures increased the pressure for results and brought an avalanche of police raids. From the start the police were faced with the difficulty of getting to grips with a section of society they found totally alien. And were they facing an organization—or an idea?

This book covers the roots of the Angry Brigade in the revolutionary ferment of the 1960s, and follows their campaign and the police investigation to its culmination in the "Stoke Newington 8" conspiracy trial at the Old Bailey—the longest criminal trial in British legal history. Written after extensive research—among both the libertarian opposition and the police—it remains the essential study of Britain's first urban guerilla group.

This expanded edition contains a comprehensive chronology of the "Angry Decade," extra illustrations and a police view of the Angry Brigade. Introductions by Stuart Christie and John Barker (two of the "Stoke Newington 8" defendants) discuss the Angry Brigade in the political and social context of its times—and its longer-term significance.

Creating a Movement with Teeth: A Documentary History of the George Jackson Brigade
edited by Daniel Burton Rose; preface by Ward Churchill

978-1-60486-223-2
$24.95

Bursting into existence in the Pacific Northwest in 1975, the George Jackson Brigade claimed 14 pipe bombings against corporate and state targets, as many bank robberies, and the daring rescue of a jailed member. Combining veterans of the prisoners' women's, gay, and black liberation movements, this organization was also ideologically diverse, consisting of both communists and anarchists. Concomitant with the Brigade's extensive armed work were prolific public communications. In more than a dozen communiqués and a substantial political statement, they sought to explain their intentions to the public while defying the law enforcement agencies that pursued them.

Collected in one volume for the first time, *Creating a Movement with Teeth* makes available this body of propaganda and mediations on praxis. In addition, the collection assembles corporate media profiles of the organization's members and alternative press articles in which partisans thrash out the heated debates sparked in the progressive community by the eruption of an armed group in their midst. *Creating a Movement with Teeth* illuminates a forgotten chapter of the radical social movements of the 1970s in which diverse interests combined forces in a potent rejection of business as usual in the United States.

Praise:
"*Creating a Movement with Teeth* is an important contribution to the growing body of literature on armed struggle in the 1970s. It gets us closer to knowing not only how pervasive militant challenges to the system were, but also the issues and contexts that shaped such strategies. Through documents by and about the George Jackson Brigade, as well as the introduction by Daniel Burton-Rose, this book sheds light on events that have until now been far too obscured."
--Dan Berger, author of *Outlaws of America: The Weather Underground and the Politics of Solidarity*; editor *The Hidden 1970s: Histories of Radicalism*.

FRIENDS OF

These are indisputably momentous times—the financial system is melting down globally and the Empire is stumbling. Now more than ever there is a vital need for radical ideas.

In the three years since its founding—and on a mere shoestring—PM Press has risen to the formidable challenge of publishing and distributing knowledge and entertainment for the struggles ahead. With over 100 releases to date, we have published an impressive and stimulating array of literature, art, music, politics, and culture. Using every available medium, we've succeeded in connecting those hungry for ideas and information to those putting them into practice.

Friends of PM allows you to directly help impact, amplify, and revitalize the discourse and actions of radical writers, filmmakers, and artists. It provides us with a stable foundation from which we can build upon our early successes and provides a much-needed subsidy for the materials that can't necessarily pay their own way. You can help make that happen – and receive every new title automatically delivered to your door once a month – by joining as a Friend of PM Press. And, we'll throw in a free T-Shirt when you sign up.

Here are your options:

• $25 a month: Get all books and pamphlets plus 50% discount on all webstore purchases.
• $25 a month: Get all CDs and DVDs plus 50% discount on all webstore purchases.
• $40 a month: Get all PM Press releases plus 50% discount on all webstore purchases
• $100 a month: Sustainer. - Everything plus PM merchandise, free downloads, and 50% discount on all webstore purchases.

For those who can't afford $25 or more a month, we're introducing Sustainer Rates at $15, $10 and $5. Sustainers get a free PM Press t-shirt and a 50% discount on all purchases from our website.

Just go to www.pmpress.org to sign up. Your Visa or Mastercard will be billed once a month, until you tell us to stop. Or until our efforts succeed in bringing the revolution around. Or the financial meltdown of Capital makes plastic redundant. Whichever comes first.

PM Press was founded at the end of 2007 by a small collection of folks with decades of publishing, media, and organizing experience. PM Press co-conspirators have published and distributed hundreds of books, pamphlets, CDs, and DVDs. Members of PM have founded enduring book fairs, spearheaded victorious tenant organizing campaigns, and worked closely with bookstores, academic conferences, and even rock bands to deliver political and challenging ideas to all walks of life. We're old enough to know what we're doing and young enough to know what's at stake.

We seek to create radical and stimulating fiction and non-fiction books, pamphlets, t-shirts, visual and audio materials to entertain, educate and inspire you. We aim to distribute these through every available channel with every available technology—whether that means you are seeing anarchist classics at our bookfair stalls; reading our latest vegan cookbook at the café; downloading geeky fiction e-books; or digging new music and timely videos from our website.

PM Press is always on the lookout for talented and skilled volunteers, artists, activists and writers to work with. If you have a great idea for a project or can contribute in some way, please get in touch.

PM PRESS
PO Box 23912
Oakland CA 94623
510-658-3906
www.pmpress.org